Krista Corbett is a new author who spent the past two years writing this book in-between working and being a mother. She grew up in BC, but now resides in Alberta, Canada with her husband and daughter. Wanting to share her own personal story with the world, Krista hopes this book to be an inspiration to others facing similar struggles and challenges.

For my late husband who pushed me to my path of self-discovery and for my husband now, who continues to keep me on track.

Krista Corbett

A WIDOW'S AWAKENING

AUSTIN MACAULEY PUBLISHERS™
LONDON • CAMBRIDGE • NEW YORK • SHARJAH

Copyright © Krista Corbett 2023

All rights reserved. No part of this publication may be reproduced, distributed, or transmitted in any form or by any means, including photocopying, recording, or other electronic or mechanical methods, without the prior written permission of the publisher, except in the case of brief quotations embodied in critical reviews and certain other non-commercial uses permitted by copyright law. For permission requests, write to the publisher.

Any person who commits any unauthorized act in relation to this publication may be liable to criminal prosecution and civil claims for damages.

All of the events in this memoir are true to the best of the author's memory. The views expressed in this memoir are solely those of the author.

Ordering Information
Quantity sales: Special discounts are available on quantity purchases by corporations, associations, and others. For details, contact the publisher at the address below.

Publisher's Cataloging-in-Publication data
Corbett, Krista
A Widow's Awakening

ISBN 9781685620783 (Paperback)
ISBN 9781685620790 (ePub e-book)

Library of Congress Control Number: 2023908498

www.austinmacauley.com/us

First Published 2023
Austin Macauley Publishers LLC
40 Wall Street, 33rd Floor, Suite 3302
New York, NY 10005
USA

mail-usa@austinmacauley.com
+1 (646) 5125767

I want to thank my parents for supporting me through my journey and my sisters for always being there to encourage me. I am also grateful to my friends who have been there for me throughout the entire writing process.

Chapter 1

Staring in silence at the lingering embers that lit up the last of the fire was an obvious sign that it was time to call it a night. We had been waiting for hours already for them to arrive, and it was almost midnight. I don't think Steven had noticed the evident silence between us that evening however apparent it was to me. I was so withdrawn from him at this point and wasn't willing to make much more of an effort. I knew this relationship would soon be coming to its end, I just didn't know exactly how soon.

As I was getting up to put out the last of the flames, I looked up toward the main road of the campground where I noticed two headlights pointed in our direction. I figured it had to be my friend, Meghan whom I had invited to come meet us for a night of camping. She had mentioned she would also be bringing along her best friend, someone I hadn't met yet.

As the lights approached our site, I could make out this retro orange Volkswagen Vanagon. My initial reaction, even before they got out of the van, was "who is this hippie she brought along." Meghan and Ben both hopped out of the van to greet us and came to join us as Steven threw some more logs on the fire. At this point, I was already quite a few drinks deep, as I needed it to endure the past few hours, contemplating if I should communicate what was going on in my mind. I had been unhappy for at least eight months already in the relationship and was finding it difficult to connect like we had at the beginning. We had a picture-perfect relationship that I had always wanted, but I was bored. I wondered if it was my lack of willingness to try and repair this otherwise doomed relationship or possibly his inability to register that there was even anything wrong. We had been together for two years and had discussed marriage, children, and a forever home, but I was only 20 and didn't understand what a commitment like that would even entail. Needless to say, the distraction of friends was very welcoming at this point.

The four of us immediately hit it off, and we ended up talking and laughing until the wee hours of the morning as we all continued to empty our coolers full of beer and cocktails.

The next morning, Steven and I had to pack up and get a move on since we both had to work that following day. We both worked for my dad; Steven as a mechanic and I as the receptionist. Meghan also worked as a service writer at my dad's car dealership, but had Mondays off, which left her and Ben to stay behind and camp another night to themselves. I didn't mind leaving since I was ready to go home and have a little space. I needed to collect my thoughts and figure out what I was finally planning on doing to end this relationship. Little did I know that there wasn't much for me to plan with the way things were about to unfold.

That next week, I went to work as per usual, but near the end of the week, I noticed a familiar vehicle pulling up in the parking lot. I was working at my dad's dealership as a receptionist and could see anyone that walked in the front doors. In came Ben, with a certain pep in his step that you couldn't ignore. It immediately caught my eye. He walked through the front doors and greeted Meghan at the service counter. I hadn't realized his intention was to come see me until Meghan filled me in after he had left. I was surprised because we really hadn't had much communication while we were camping, but over the next couple weeks he started to show up randomly for quick visits. He had been expressing his interest in me to Meghan, who had been filling me in. I wasn't really sure how to react because it felt like it just came out of nowhere, but it was starting to feel like a way out of my current relationship. My relationship at that point felt like it was doomed to end one way or another. I had been longing to feel loved and adored for years through my adolescents and Steven was the first one to fit that mold. After two years together, I was beginning to realize there just wasn't anything there between us but the initial attraction with no depth.

A few weeks later, after work one night, some of the staff and I went to a local billiards hall to have dinner and play some pool, and I suggested to Meghan that she invite Ben. A few hours later, Ben showed up, and the entire night I felt a powerful connection for the first time that I couldn't explain. Throughout the night, we were laughing, teasing each other, and flirting. I knew that something felt different about him, but I couldn't put my finger on it.

The next weekend, I went with Meghan and Steven and a few other friends to a nightclub, where I was trying my best to avoid Steven most of the night. I knew Ben was planning to show up at some point and was feeling really excited about seeing him again. When he finally did, it was like the two of us were magnetic to each other. We spent an hour in the back of the club attached to each other, but also aware that I had to be careful not to be too obviously interested in him because Steven was still in the vicinity and would pick up on it. I don't know who couldn't have. I had never been drawn to someone so instantly in my life. It was after midnight when everyone was thinking of making their way home when I suggested that "Meghan" take me home. Steven wanted me to come with him, but I quickly made up an excuse about wanting to sleep in my own bed, and he accepted the excuse and said I would see him the next day. I was still living at home with my parents, so I knew he wouldn't know if I wasn't heading home right away anyway. Meghan, Ben and I all jumped into his dark grey Ford F150 and drove Meghan to drop her off so Ben and I could continue our conversation and get to know each other a little better. We drove to my neighborhood and parked in the parking lot above the park just down the street. The gates are always closed at this time of the night, however, this night they were open in an almost seeming invitation for us. We sat for hours in the wee hours of the morning talking about our dreams, desires, music, passions, and everything that we could find out about each other. We had so much in common, and there was an instant connection that felt like electricity. I had never felt so emotionally bonded to a person after only spending a few hours with them. We eventually kissed, which felt like 1000 butterflies flittering around in my chest. I knew it was wrong, but it felt like this was the beginning of the rest of my life. I felt like I was writing a new fairytale. A love story.

Ben dropped me off as the sun was beginning to rise, and I went straight to bed. It was early morning, and I slept until almost noon, and when I woke up, my first thought was of him. I tried to recall the events of the night before and wondered if it was real or just a dream. The feelings I had for him were so strong in just a short time. It was lust. I was so in lust with someone I barely knew, and I felt guilty because I still had a boyfriend. I met up with Ben that afternoon and we spent the night at a friend of mine's home, and were completely attached to each other. We were all over each other and couldn't take a finger off one another. It felt like the right thing to go to Steven's and end our two-year relationship. It was such a whirlwind the last week and I knew I was ready to break it off. This past week was the push that I needed. Without hesitation, I left in a hurry, wanting to break things off so I could be free of guilt to be with Ben. I had no emotional responsibility to Steven anymore and was ready to break the bond.

It was late when I showed up and immediately dived in to explain that we were over, completely unaware of how out of the blue this must have been for him as he begged me to stay and explain why I was doing this. The way I learned to deal with situations like this was to shut myself off emotionally and not to ingest any of his grievances and let him deal with them on his own. It was no longer my problem, and I was happy to walk out of his house and not look back. My future was now with Ben, even though I was oblivious to how chaotic and destructive it was about to become.

Those next few weeks created some confusion for me. We were so inseparable at times, and then other times I couldn't reach him for days. One night, I had a party at my parent's house with a group of my friends, and he promised to be there. It was late when he actually showed up, wide-eyed and drunk. I had no idea where he had been previously, but I brushed it aside because I was so excited to actually see him and introduce him to some friends. I can recall some friends suspicious of him being on drugs, specifically cocaine, because he was fidgeting and acting strangely. I again brushed this off as I was in such a state of lust. Not long after he arrived, he took off, and again, I didn't know where he had gone. I tried calling and texting but didn't get a reply. I was starting to get annoyed as he finally replied; he said he had gone to his truck where he had parked up the street to make a few phone calls. This struck me as odd as I hadn't been exposed to this kind of behavior before, since none of my friends did drugs. It was mostly just social drinking that many of us explored in our teens and early twenties. That night, I passed out after consuming too many vodka sodas and woke up to a half dozen missed calls from Ben. Apparently, he had come back to the house in the early hours of the morning, knocking on my bedroom window trying to wake me, but I was in a deep drunk sleep. This hurt me to my core. I was so disappointed that he hadn't made me a priority that night, especially around my friends and especially after how much we had connected and gotten so close in such a short period of time. I didn't understand and was so unaware of the activity he was up to, and I felt like I immediately needed to protect myself from getting hurt. I could see it coming. Everything was happening at lightning speed, and I couldn't slow the feelings down. That was the start of knowing that I had to protect my emotions and show him that he couldn't hurt me. I couldn't let him see how his actions that night had affected me on such a deep level. What was even more surprising to me though was the fact that he had hurt me so much just from ditching me that night before.

As the weeks went on, when we made plans, he wouldn't show. We discussed going out of town only an hour away, but he cancelled at the last minute. We booked a cabin up in a remote location just outside of town, and I didn't hear from him until late in the day we were supposed to check in. I didn't know where he was or what he was doing. Finally, I got fed up and went to his house to demand an explanation. He was living with his parents, and I found his bedroom window where I began banging on it to get his attention. I could see he was in bed, covers over top of him, and I don't know how he could've slept through the banging, because he didn't move an inch. I wondered why he was even in such a deep sleep at three in the afternoon. I knew he was a pretty heavy pot smoker but couldn't understand why he was in a comatose sleep so late in the day. I left, defeated without answers. I was angry but also wasn't going to let him see how he had hurt me again. I was taking this extremely personal as I struggled with fear of rejection. I had struggled with this growing up and was starting to feel like he was rejecting me, which confused me even more.

That evening, he called me, apologizing profusely once again. I told him it was fine, and he agreed to come over to see me later that night. When he got to my house, he admitted that he had driven the entire hour long drive up to the cabin that night before we were supposed to go and had left cutout hearts on several trees with our initials on them. I wasn't sure if I should believe him, but it was such a romantic gesture, I chose to forgive him immediately and was sorry I didn't get to see them. He told me he had spent the entire night trying to profess his adoration for me, so he was tired the next day, and couldn't get out of bed for our trip. Again, this was strange behavior to me, but I accepted it and all I cared about was him being near me at this time and enjoying the moment that he was actually there.

This unusual behavior didn't stop, and I was getting more and more irritated, hurt and felt rejected. We both partied a lot during those six weeks, and we even exchanged the "love" word between each other one night not long after we started dating. It wasn't long before I started to realize that my style of partying was different. I couldn't understand why he could stay up so late, sleep all day, and repeat this over and over. I was so oblivious to the effects of what drugs were capable of doing to a person. Finally, one last evening, he broke a promise to come to see me and I had had enough. I wasn't going to wait around for him forever and continue to get my heart broken. I knew this wasn't a normal relationship and had to break it off. We agreed to meet near my girlfriend's house, and surprisingly, he showed up. I hopped into his truck, ready to tell him I was done. I wanted to hurt him the way he had been continually hurting me for the past weeks. Before I could say anything, he explained that he didn't think we should continue dating. I was shocked and instantly once again felt rejected. I was crushed and my heart sank. I wanted to be the one to hurt him back, so he knew how it felt. Instead, he was once again stabbing me in the chest emotionally, and I couldn't show my grief. I didn't want to give him the satisfaction. I thought it was some sick game he was playing me for. I truly felt like I loved him at this point but had to walk away as gracefully as I could, so I didn't get sucked into feeling like the victim. I was stronger than that. It seemed so easy for him to do, and I walked away from him with my head held high until I got into my car and wept. There were so many emotions over the last six weeks, feelings that I had never felt before, and it all came to a halt that afternoon, no fault of my own. I was devastated and needed some comfort from my friend, so I went and was consoled by her that afternoon.

Life continued over those next couple of months. I got a new job at a liquor store; I tried to forget as best as I could about the six weeks prior. I had heard nothing from Ben but had heard from Meghan that he had been checked into the local hospital and admitted to the psych ward. He had been using cocaine heavily, combined with marijuana and alcohol, and was addicted to all three. He was admitted to the hospital until there was a bed available at an addiction treatment facility, where he would be discharged to. I don't think I was overly surprised at this; mostly I was surprised at the fact that he had hid so much from me, seeing as how close emotionally we had become in the previous months before. One night, when I was working an evening shift at the liquor store, I decided to run next door to the gas station for a few items. I opened the door to see Ben bending over the gum selection, oblivious that I had just entered. My heart started pounding and I could feel the heat radiating off my face. I was not good with confrontation and my immediate reaction was to run away. I quickly turned and headed out the door as fast as I could without him seeing me. I scanned the parking lot and saw his parents in the vehicle waiting for him. He must have gotten a pass at the hospital that night. I knew the hospital allowed this if he was chaperoned. I couldn't and was not ready to face him. I'd had zero communication with him, let alone seen him, and I wouldn't have known what to say. A million thoughts ran through my head. Whether or not to run back and say something or maybe demand an explanation, but I couldn't risk the fear of being rejected again. I got back to the liquor store and watched the vehicle drive away as my heart pounded. They were most likely headed back to the hospital, and I wondered if that was going to be the last time, I ever saw him.

After a few weeks, I received a phone call from Ben's mom, Brenda. She was calling to fill me in on where Ben had been admitted, which was a treatment center on Vancouver Island. It was an unexpected phone call, but welcome and reassuring. I felt touched that she knew the importance of me to Ben, and that she had taken the time to call and let me know. She explained that he would be in the center for at least two months. I was grateful that she had reached out, even though I wondered if I would ever talk to him again. I assumed he must have asked her to call, which gave me a glimpse of hope and fear at the same time. Life carried on and I waited four weeks before I heard anything from him, and the first attempt at communication was a letter addressed to myself from him. I wasn't expecting any communication until he was out of rehab, let alone a letter in the mail. I thought it was so old fashioned but romantic nonetheless. Immediately, I tore into the letter and devoured every word he wrote as if he were in front of me. My heart was filled with emotion and that was the first sign that he still cared about me and that I hadn't imagined the love that I felt for him before he had broken my heart and left. I wrote him back, thinking that it was such a vintage form of communication, but I didn't care. I don't think I have ever been so excited to check the mailbox in my life. We spent the next couple weeks writing back and forth, and finally, on Christmas Eve, my phone rang from an undisclosed number, and I wasn't going to answer it at first. I thought it must have been a telemarketer, but when I heard him on the line, I began to shake. My palms got sweaty, and I ran downstairs to hide in my closet for some privacy. He only had a few minutes to chat, but I couldn't bear the thought of not hearing his voice. It was a brief conversation, but I was happy to hear from him, and he promised he would try back within the week. I don't think I left my phone outside of my view for the next few weeks. We were still writing each other back and forth via mail, and the more we communicated, the more I felt like it was destined for us to be together. I had no doubt in my mind that he felt the same way about me and we would reconnect once he was finished with his treatment.

That winter, I had been planning a mission trip with my mom in the New Year to Mexico. I knew I wouldn't be able to communicate with him during that time, but I still continued to write to him so I could feel that connection even though we were countries apart. It was such a chaotic time in our family at that point, because my dad was starting to drink heavily and we had just found out that my younger sister, who was only 17, was experimenting with cocaine also. My mom was hesitant to even go on this trip, but we had already committed, and she planned to deal with the family situation when we got back. We were gone for two weeks, and I don't think there was a day that went by without me thinking about Ben. I was so distracted with my feelings for him that I wasn't paying attention to the coming deterioration of my parents' marriage and the addiction that was overtaking my sister's early adolescent life. All I could focus on was getting through the next couple weeks because Ben was finishing up his last couple weeks of treatment and would be home soon after we got back from our trip.

It was February 2007 when I got a call that he would be coming home. I couldn't focus on much that day because I was too excited and anxious. His parents were going to pick him up and bring him home, and I was hoping he wouldn't waste a minute to see me. I drove aimlessly around town for hours because I knew as soon as he called me, I would rush to his house to reunite with my soul mate. My parents lived at least a 20-minute drive from him, so I figured I would wait closer to his house so I would be able to drive straight there and see him. When I got the call, I could sense the excitement in his voice. I drove straight there, ran to the door and knocked. I can remember this image vividly. As I stood knocking on the front steps, I heard him flying down the stairs to the front door. He opened the door, and we rushed instantly into each other's arms without closing the door. I was so relieved that he felt the same excitement that I did to see and feel him. I was shaking as we sat down to relish in each other, mainly because I was so overwhelmed with excitement and emotion. I noticed he had put on some weight, which I thought was charming. It was because he had actually been eating in treatment and wasn't skin and bones when he first got admitted. After we had reunited once again, I went over to greet his parents, who had graciously given us our time together. We went to his room and spent the next few hours savoring each other's company and enjoying the time we had together once again. It felt amazing to be near him, hold his hand and be given the affection I had longed for months from him. I stayed as long as his parents would allow, as he was on a strict schedule having been so newly released from treatment. We promised each other that we would reconnect the next day and left each other dreaming about our futures that felt like they were actually possible this time around.

Chapter 2

Ben had been doing so well those first few months. He was attending his AA meetings, working with his sponsor, and working the 12-step program that they taught him at treatment. He seemed so full of life and was teaching me all he had learned about feelings, emotions, and the self-awareness around how he was feeling at a specific time. This was so new to me because I had always stuffed my feelings growing up and wouldn't allow myself to show any weakness, which back then meant showing sadness, fear, or vulnerability. I don't know how and when I became so habitual about keeping everything inside and not allowing myself to show any kind of emotion. I was so shut off. By the time I had met Ben, I had been that way for years.

Thinking back, I suppose it started at some point in high school. I was part of the popular crowd, but I felt like I was always trying to compete for attention, like I had to prove myself somehow in order to be accepted. Not being part of the "in" crowd was just not good enough for me. I had some of my best friends in that group that I will always have and will always cherish those friendships, but I still often wonder if I was being true to myself even with them.

When I look back and recall my moments of emotional unavailability, I think back to a student that attended my school who was a couple years older than me and had passed away. The school held an assembly in her memory for the rest of the students who were shocked at her passing. I can remember a few friends of mine who were in tears, and I just couldn't understand why they were so upset. I didn't know this girl well, and I knew they didn't either, so I was confused as to why they were so emotional over it.

Looking back now, I can understand why it was such a sad day, because our school was fairly small, and she was in my older sister's grade and would have graduated with her in a few years to come. Everyone knew who she was, so it hit a lot of people close to home that one of their peers had become ill and was suddenly gone.

This self-inflicting habit carried on with me for years until I met Ben. Once he was out of treatment, he taught me to be open to recognize my anger, excitement, or other emotions I was feeling and that it was OK to express them. Every day, he would start by asking me how I was doing or feeling, and if I replied "good," he would correct me and say "good" was not a feeling.

I began to adapt to this new self-aware technique and we began to connect on an even deeper level. He was bringing out more enlightenment in me that I didn't even know existed. I had been operating a certain way for such a long time, and he was opening me up. It was a scary feeling, but it was also such a weight being lifted off me. He was so healthy in his mind and spirit, and I was on my own journey to catch up.

As Ben worked his program diligently, I watched as my dad began to do the opposite. My mom and dad were fighting daily at this point, which encouraged my mom to organize her own intervention to try to get Dad some help. I truly believe that Ben's parents came into our lives for a reason because his mom was coaching my mom through the same experience she had just gone through with Ben. My mom was at a loss and hadn't had any other support at that time concerning addiction. She guided my mom to a woman who specialized in interventions and who would facilitate an intervention at our home to get Dad off to treatment.

I wasn't fully aware of my dad's drinking habits at this point in my life, as I wasn't home much to witness most of it. I do remember being embarrassed when he would black out when we would have our friends over, stumbling and spilling his drinks while slurring and falling down the stairs. I didn't think this was entirely abnormal behavior because I watched many of my own friends act that way at parties. I just assumed he was letting loose and releasing some steam. The part I wasn't paying attention to, though, was how it had accelerated in the last few months and how it was affecting our family and his business.

My mom was quick to book the interventionist, and the morning that she arrived, we were all sitting in the living room as a family, waiting for my dad to come down the stairs. The plan was to each read to him a letter we had written individually, expressing how his alcoholism had been affecting us.

I have three sisters, and two of them were present, along with myself. We were all there except my sister, Maddy who refused to be part of it. I always believed that she had decided to not partake in the intervention because she was in the cycle of her own addiction with drugs and alcohol herself and maybe felt that it might be a little too close for comfort for her.

At his usual time, Dad came down the stairs ready to eat some breakfast before work when he noticed us all sitting and waiting for him. The interventionist invited him into the living room to explain to him what was happening. She took the lead and started explaining why we were all there, and invited us each to read our personal letters directed to Dad. I must have been learning something from Ben about emotions, because when I started reading my letter, I couldn't hold back the tears. I must have had so much pent-up sadness and grief seeing my dad in such a painful state that I just let it pour out. I was realizing I hadn't even processed the effect his behaviors were having on me and my family. It didn't hit me until I started reading my letter. I could feel things that I hadn't allowed myself to feel for a very long time. It was a release to allow myself to let it all come out; verbally, physically and emotionally. We all read our letters as we sobbed together, and eventually, Dad agreed to go to treatment. He would have to leave that very day, as they had a plane ticket booked for him. This wouldn't allow any time for him to change his mind. He would be going for a minimum of two months to get the help and the basic foundation he needed for his recovery. My mom would have to take over the business temporarily to get things back on track because the business had suffered immensely from his lack of attention and diligence as he succumbed slowly to his addiction.

After about an hour of going around the room with each one of us explaining why and how his drinking had been affecting us, he reluctantly agreed to get some help. Once the decision had been made, he packed his bags for the same treatment facility Ben had just come home from and hopped on a plane after downing as many beers as he could consume because after that day, he may never see or touch another drink again.

During Dad's stay in treatment, Ben would fill me in on what Dad might be experiencing during his stay there. Ben had just been through the same regime months before, and he helped me understand the day-to-day that my dad might be going through. At Edgewood, they had family days at the treatment center, so after about a month, my two younger sisters and I piled into the car with my mom to make the drive out to Vancouver Island to see how Dad had been doing. I was curious to see where Ben had spent the past couple months and to also check in on Dad. We only got to spend the Sunday afternoon with him because they had a strict policy for visitors and a strict schedule at the center. Dad seemed to be doing better. He seemed more humbled and more at peace. He was present with us during our time together, something I hadn't experienced much of over my childhood years. We finally had a branch of hope that he would come back home a different person.

We left that next week, and I was ready to get back to Ben. That was the first time since he'd been back home that I'd been apart from him for longer than a few days, and it was tough. I felt that it was a good experience, however, because the visit to Edgewood connected me to him that much more.

During the next month of my dad's stay at Edgewood, Ben and I continued to plan our future together. I, too, was committed to staying sober to support him, which meant zero alcohol for me also. I had never been committed to staying sober for any length of time before that. Even back in my high school days, my girlfriends and I were going out to the nightclubs long before we were of legal age. We would hide in one of my girlfriend's bedrooms and drink anything we could mix with vodka to get a decent buzz on and head out to the clubs. This happened plenty through the weeks and more on weekends. I would borrow my older sister's I.D. since I was still two years underage. Not only was I reckless about going out underage to bars and night clubs, but the daring behavior I was displaying could have easily led to more dangerous situations. We would casually jump into cars with men we wouldn't know for rides, end up at drug houses where you never really knew if the cops were going to show up at any given time, and black out on multiple occasions, forgetting exactly how I got home, only to find my vehicle that I must have driven home in the driveway.

This seemed to become a perpetual habit in Grade 12, my final year of high school. I wouldn't show up to my classes in the mornings after our late-night escapades of partying, and eventually my dad would come looking for me at the school since they'd received word that I wasn't in attendance again. I would typically make up some lame excuse that I wasn't feeling well and left or had overslept at my friend's house.

This alcohol abuse had become a pattern of heavy drinking at the time I was 15. I still remember the details of the first time I got drunk. Most of the time, the way to get booze bought for you if you were underage was to hang out around the local liquor store and wait until you saw someone who looked like they might buy for you. Other times, we would send in one of our friends who looked the oldest, and if they didn't get ID'd, we would toast and drink to our success. That night, on my first drunk experience, we were successful. I shared a 2L of peach cider with my friend, and we headed across the street to go hang out in front of the 7/11 convenience store with a group of buddies. Eventually, we made it to the sand pits, an area where most bush parties were held with a bonfire and zero chaperones. It didn't take me long to discover the warm sensation that crept throughout my body and the level of confidence I had found from a bottle.

Now, at this time in my life, even though I enjoyed drinking, I was ultimately committed to Ben. I had exchanged one infatuation for the next and withholding from drinking didn't seem like a big deal at the time. My intoxication came from him. I loved the feeling more than anything else, just being in his presence.

One night, a few weeks into our committed sobriety, it was a friend's birthday and I was invited to go. I was hesitant because I didn't know how Ben would feel about it, but he convinced me to go if I didn't plan on drinking. I had no intention of drinking, because I knew how this would affect him and our relationship. That night, I didn't follow the plan. I got completely obliterated and ended up waking up in my bed, completely unaware of how I had gotten there the night before. The last thing I can remember was standing in line for shots with my friends at the bar, like it was just a normal Saturday night. I wasn't even in control of how much I was drinking. It was like I was in another world once the alcohol kicked in and there was no turning back. I woke up feeling an unavoidable pang of guilt that I had really messed up. I knew Ben would be extremely disappointed, and I was overwhelmingly disappointed in myself. I knew I'd messed up, and I needed the security of knowing that he would forgive me. When we spoke on the phone, I could hear the disapproval in his voice. He agreed to let me come to his house, and I quickly got myself together and drove there as fast as I could handle being in the state I was in. I could barely keep from vomiting as I drove, and every bump or turn made me nauseous. I was struggling to keep from shaking from the withdrawals and dehydration. I'd been there many times before, but I never had anyone hold me to this new standard I wasn't used to. I was so angry at myself. I had put my own wants first and hadn't even considered how this might affect his recovery.

I pulled up to his parents' house, and I couldn't even make it to the side door before I let everything come out of my stomach. I wasn't about to show my face to his parents in this condition. I felt the nausea rising in my throat. I found the closest shrub and hurled myself into it. If only he had seen what I had done. I couldn't bear the thought of even telling him. I covered it up and sheepishly made my way through the basement door and to his room. I could tell on his face how dismayed and hurt he was at my behavior.

That was a turning point for me, in which I vowed to never drink again in order to support him and his sobriety entirely. I knew the consequences of my actions, and all I could do was try to gain his trust back. I was sober for eight months straight after that.

After two full months in treatment, dad came back from Edgewood and seemed to be doing really well for a while. He was more present, more loving and just seemed to be happier overall. It seemed like he had really done a lot of self-work at the treatment facility, and it was nice to see him and my mom getting along so well. I don't remember a time when they were really connected the way they were then. My mom was always extremely strict with us growing up, and my dad was more laid back, which caused plenty of conflict in their marriage and our family. My sisters and I were pretty rebellious in our teens, which probably led us to the drinking and drugs that went along with the uncompromising rules and regulations in our home. Out of spite, I used to open my bedroom window, which was right next to my parents' bedroom and light a joint at the time I was only 15, or I would sneak out of the house to go party when my mom had grounded me. We were constantly at war with my mom. My older sister moved out when she was only 17 since my mom and her were constantly arguing. She would often punch holes through the wall in frustration, and there would frequently be a screaming match going on. We were always fighting with her for more freedom. I think we were always trying to test my mom to see how far we could push it. There was absolutely no give with her, so it didn't matter how far we could take it because there would always be consequences to be had.

Before our house burned down in the catastrophic Okanagan Mountain Park fire in 2003, I then had my own bedroom in the basement in which the window was ground level. I used to sneak in my boyfriend at the time through the window and we would have sex while my dad was in the next room watching television. No one was ever the wiser, until our plumbing got backed up one day. My mom had to call the plumber in, and he found multiple condoms that had been flushed down the toilet coming from my own bathroom, which had caused a backup in the sewer system. My mom knew it was me, and I thought I was going to be grounded forever. There was no shortage of drama in our family of four teenage girls as we were continually fighting for our freedom against our parents.

That spring faded into summer and Ben and I continued to spend every waking moment together that we could. We decided to move in together, which was not recommended in his recovery program. In AA, they say not to make any big decisions in the first year of your recovery. We made a lot of big decisions in that first six months of his recovery, let alone first year.

Moving in together was amazing. I loved the thought of going to sleep every night and waking up beside him each morning. The first month that we spent in our apartment was heaven. I couldn't remember a time that I had been as happy as then. That summer, Ben had lost his driver's license due to some charges that had been laid while he was in treatment. I hadn't been fully aware of the charges against him, but while he was in treatment, I did see his mug shot that came up online as one of Kelowna's wanted criminals. I had no idea while he was in treatment what had led him to these charges, but once he was back home, he explained to me the situation and what he was up against. When he had been initially admitted into the psych ward, he was heavily doing drugs and was selling them also. I don't recall if he was actually charged for this, but one of the other charges he was facing was for theft. He had been stealing license plates and filling up his vehicle with a tank full of fuel then taking off before he had to pay. This was long before you had to pre pay for fuel. The service station attendants would never catch him because he always had a stolen license plate, but what the police caught on camera from one of these stunts had apparently linked him to another crime that he had committed. One night, just before I had met him, he had been high on cocaine and was looking for a quick way to earn some fast cash. He took a knife and walked into a local gas station and held up the store at knife point. He ran away with only a few hundred dollars. The police must have gotten his truck on camera and linked the two offences and were after him. The reason that he had been advertised on the wanted list was because he had failed to appear in court on the scheduled date. He had been treated at the time of his scheduled court hearing, however, and they allowed him to reschedule his court date when he returned. I didn't find this out until I was already committed to him, and nothing of this sort was going to stand in our way anyway. Little did I know that there would be many more bombs coming my way that I would have to learn to accept.

During the time he had failed to have his driver's license, he was taking the transit system to get to work. He wasn't happy about it, but we managed to get through it. The summer we lived together went by in a flash. One Saturday in the middle of July, we had just returned home from a getaway to Tofino when he proposed to me in the middle of the lake on rented jet skis. At first, I thought he was breaking up with me by the way he began to express his feelings about our relationship, and I could feel my heart was sinking. I felt a lump in my throat as he was describing our relationship, and then just as I thought he was going to say it, he pulled out a beautiful one-carat diamond solitaire ring. We had gone to the jewelers a few times before just to browse rings, and he remembered the one that I was eyeing, although I thought it would have been months before he could afford it. The lawyer fees had been accumulating on top of all the criminal fees he had to pay to get rid of his record, so I couldn't believe he had done this. I immediately accepted and couldn't believe that we were engaged. He was officially my fiancé. I was going to marry my soul mate. We went straight to my parents' and showed off my ring to everyone as we basked in our engagement bliss. As if moving in together wasn't fast enough, just a few months out of rehab and we were already living together and engaged. We were two lost souls that were counting on each other to get through life on the basis that our fairytale devotion of one another would carry us to eternity.

That summer came and went, and by fall, I could tell Ben was beginning to struggle with his recovery and following his program. I don't believe that he missed the drugs quite as much as the alcohol, but as I saw my friends continuing to enjoy and socialize in their early twenties, I started to feel the first touch of loneliness and resentment. It wasn't yet a deep resentment that had built up, but I was starting to feel like the distance I had put between my friends, and I wasn't exactly fair since I didn't think I was the one with the addiction issues. During this time that I was trying to understand how to support Ben in staying sober while I myself struggled. My dad had begun drinking again as he wasn't following his recovery program like he should have which caused a problem for Ben. The problem with watching my dad not follow his program and "getting away" with drinking had a big influence on Ben's wanting to dip his feet back into that pool of dangerous endeavors.

He really wasn't seeing the whole story, though. My dad was coming home from work, secretly pouring vodka into his orange juice after my mom had gone to bed and was hiding the evidence in the garage. He began doing this on a regular basis over the following months, and it wasn't long before we were all starting to catch on. One night, I showed up at the house after Mom had gone to bed and found Dad sitting on the couch with a full drink in hand, slurring his speech. I soon realized this was his nightly routine. After everyone had gone to bed each night, he would pour himself a stiff drink and plant himself on the couch in the basement and watch his music DVDs until he would either pass out or stumble up to his bedroom. We started to become aware of the drinking when he began to become more emotionally closed off and not work his 12-step program that they taught at Edgewood. Dad wouldn't admit to having started drinking again, but we all knew what was going on. The night that I showed up later in the evening to find out the truth, I was searching through possible hiding locations in the garage and came across an empty vodka bottle he had stashed away in his hockey gear bag. This was the evidence I needed to prove to my mom that he had relapsed. I didn't want to have to show this to my mom and go through the chaos again, but we had already been living in the chaos whether we wanted to acknowledge it or not.

This was the beginning of my parents' separation, along with more evidence that my mom had found out that rocked her to her core. It was a Wednesday night when my dad told my mom that he would be going out of town that next night for a work trip. My mom knew exactly what that could lead to. Although my mom had begged him not to go, Dad refused and looked her straight in the eye and said he was leaving without any hesitation. That next day, Dad left and Mom carried on with her day with a sick feeling in the pit of her stomach that she couldn't shake. She called him that evening to ask if he'd gotten a room with a mini bar, and he answered yes. Her heart sank. She then asked if he had opened anything, and she knew he was lying through his teeth when he answered no. They hung up the phone and there was a feeling of despair and surrender as she remembered a journal he had written in rehab that he demanded her never to touch. With him out of the house, she reluctantly headed for their bedroom where he kept this untouchable journal and began to flip through pages and pages of listed infidelities he had had over the past 13 years. This exercise was part of one of the steps in AA that requires you to write out a moral inventory of all your actions, thoughts and emotions that lead you down your path of addiction. My dad had always gone away for work over the years as a part of his career, and my mom had said she had always wondered if there were ever other women he had been involved with. My dad was extremely convincing as he would kneel down beside her, take her hand in his, and promise to her that he had never been with any other woman during their 25-year marriage. As she read through these guilty accounts of multiple affairs and betrayals, she sobbed as she knew this was the final straw that had been broken in their marriage. This news had obviously shocked my mom and left her questioning everything. Over the past 6 months, my mom had been committed to learning about addiction and going to regular Coda meetings. CODA stands for "Co Dependents

Anonymous." She had been learning that in order to actually help my dad, she could no longer be dependent on him. It wasn't just my mom that was appalled by this new information; our entire family was devastated. Not only did this information affect my mom but my sisters and I were also extremely hurt and confused. I had always believed that my dad was faithful to my mom because we were raised in a Christian household. Growing up, we went to church every Sunday morning and attended Sunday school regularly. I grew up believing that if you are a Christian, you should follow the commandments of the Bible. Being as strict as my mom was, I wouldn't have dared guess that my dad would have broken the most crucial commandment for a marriage: Thou shalt not commit adultery. None of us were surprised when my mom told my dad to leave after the findings of his cheating combined with his unwillingness to work on his recovery. Soon after, Dad found a condo to rent and moved his things out that week.

I always wondered if he subconsciously wanted my mom to find that journal, seeing as he had mentioned it to her and didn't put much effort into hiding it. Maybe he was relieved that he didn't have the responsibility of carrying on a marriage that he clearly wasn't committed to or that he could now carry on with whatever antics he so chose. His drinking almost immediately got worse once he moved out on his own.

Ben continued to struggle more and more with his sobriety and my dad's drinking continued to get worse. My dad and Ben had always had a certain connection between them, and they had mutual respect for one another. Maybe it was the addict in them that connected them both. Ben was adopted as a baby and had always said that he had a connection with my dad in ways that he'd not had with his adoptive father. One of the reasons for his struggles that led to alcohol abuse was the fact that he had been adopted and hadn't had the opportunity to meet his birth parents. I knew he had wanted to find his birth mother, but it never materialized. I think it was his fear of rejection and not knowing how to cope if it ever came to that. His parents loved him unconditionally, there was no mistaking that, but I don't know if he was ever honest with them about how his being adopted had greatly affected him mentally. He had mentioned that he had issues with rejection, even growing up as a child stemming from his birth mother turning him over to the adoption agency.

I felt like my entire life was being consumed by alcohol and the addictions of Ben, my dad, and my sister, who was still doing cocaine and drinking heavily. I was trying to support Ben's sobriety, even though he was getting closer and closer to having that first relapse, while trying to support my mom through her separation and not knowing what to do with my sister. It was a heavy load for me as I was only 21 and I knew the chaos couldn't last forever. I was trying to be strong, but eventually it would have to give way.

That fall, Ben and I made another big decision. My career was just getting started and I was working as a realtor on a team of four agents and we had just listed a great investment property. Together, Ben and I decided that we would purchase this home, build a secondary home on the oversized lot, then turn it around and flip it to make a profit. The market was so hot in Kelowna in 2007. A lot of investors were taking advantage of the real estate market and we knew we had an advantage to make some money since I was an active realtor and Ben was a journeyman carpenter. The plan was to build a secondary dwelling within a six-month time frame and then list the property to hopefully make a decent profit. My dad was the one who invested the capital in the project in order for us to pay for the labor and materials. Ben had a hard time maintaining jobs and had spontaneously walked off a job site just before we got possession of the home. We figured this freed him up to spend a minimum of 40 hours per week on this project. He was in charge of building it while I was still working as a realtor.

October came and we were getting packed and organized to move into our first home together when we found our third member of the family, Koda. She was a two-year-old Rottweiler who was extremely aggressive upon our first meeting with her, but we figured she would become familiar with us quickly enough and she would be a perfect guard dog. We knew we wanted a Rottweiler, and even though she was foaming at the mouth when we went to go meet her, we still fell in love. She was like a misunderstood creature who needed a good home and love. Ben brought her home the week that we moved into our new home, and she easily adapted to us. She did, however, take longer to adapt to her surroundings and the new people that came around the house. Even still, we welcomed her into our home with open arms and loved her unconditionally. She was like the third piece of our puzzle. Life was just about bliss at this point. We had our home, we had our family, and we had a plan.

That winter, the planning of the carriage home took longer than we expected. We didn't have much of a plan for finances and banked on the fact that we would be making a big enough profit when we sold the property that we would just have to make it through the six months we estimated it would take us. We both didn't have any concept of what owning a home really entailed and the cost of a mortgage with insurance and utility bills. I was relying heavily on Ben to finish the project within our proposed time frame because I didn't think my wages alone could carry us through. Without him earning an income, it would be tight during the building process, and we were extremely uneducated on the amount of money this would require.

The plans to begin building were stalled as we needed permits from the city, which we didn't account for time wise, so we decided it would be a good idea to do a little renovating in the main home that we were living in. This house was a 1940s heritage home and hadn't been updated for years. It had the original hardwood floors and crystal vintage doorknobs that gave the home its character. It was quaint and in a neighborhood that was surrounded by similar style homes close to downtown and the beach. There was so much potential with this home, and we figured that a little paint, kitchen cabinets, and bathroom would add nothing but value. Ben began the demolition and renovations within a few weeks of moving in, and pretty soon we were living in a construction zone. We were not prepared in the least for what we were putting on ourselves within Ben's first year out of treatment. We were making all the big decisions that Edgewood had shied us away from, which could lead to a relapse. We didn't even consider rethinking any of it. We had the belief that our love would pull us through any hard times we might encounter. We just didn't realize the severity of the hard times that lay ahead. As if moving wasn't stressful enough, we were adding a renovation budget to the building expense, living in a 950 sq ft home that was completely torn apart, with a lack of income and still trying to stay sober. This was all while we were in the process of beginning to think about plans for our wedding next spring.

No wonder in the AA program, they advise not to make any big decisions within the year of getting out of treatment. We completely went against this advice and made some of the biggest decisions of our lives that would change our lives completely.

Chapter 3

It was the middle of a cold and depressing December, and we were driving home one evening from Ben' parents' house when we passed a liquor store. I was surprised when he suggested that we stop and get something to drink. It was so out of nowhere and I was very uncomfortable at the thought of supporting his relapse, but I didn't fully comprehend the consequences it might have brought. After a few minutes of convincing me, I succumbed to the thought that maybe we could start small and have a few drinks together, but if it got out of hand, we would both agree to stop immediately. I believe, looking back now, that this decision was the one that would shape the rest of our time together, and I was in complete denial of how this would affect the manipulation and struggle that we were about to face. My agreeing to purchase this first bottle of liquor in the past eight months would also shape the way Ben was able to manipulate me entirely. I was still so young and didn't have any kind of guidebook or experience with living with a recovering alcoholic and drug addict. I knew we were both stressed to the max and thought that maybe it wouldn't hurt, and in a way, I think I wanted to let off some steam and be able to be a normal 21-year-old again.

I can recall pulling up to the liquor store and browsing the sections of beer, liquor, wine, and cider. We grabbed a 12 pack of beer and a 2'6 bottle of vodka with some chase.

This clearly was not "starting out small." We brought it back to the house, and I could sense Ben's excitement and eagerness to dip into that familiar feeling that he'd been longing for quite some time. I was still very apprehensive about it but was counting on Ben to keep his promise if anything got out of hand.

As the night went on, it seemed like a pretty normal evening, much like one that I had known to have with friends. I was anticipating him acting the way he had before treatment, and expected him to hop in his truck and take off to who knew where. This had been my experience when I was with him prior to him getting sober, so I didn't know if this behavior would begin again

That night, it got late quickly, and I knew it was time for me to go to bed after starting to stumble and slur a little, and I passed out in the bedroom sometime before midnight. I couldn't have been asleep for more than a couple hours when I woke up to find an empty space beside me on the bed. I knew it had to be sometime early in the morning but I was groggy from drinking too many vodkas sodas. I peeked out the bedroom door to find Ben sitting at the dining room table, head down, holding a half-empty bottle of beer. It startled me to find the empty case of beer sitting on the floor next to the table. He drank every bottle, which was a huge amount to consume after having zero alcohol in his system for the past 11 months. I went over to him to find out if he would be coming to bed, and I could see anger on his face. I didn't understand why he had gotten so upset, until he began mumbling about taking on more than he could handle. He went on about how he didn't know how to build this house, and he wouldn't be able to do it. His anger escalated quickly as I tried to ease him. The more he spoke about it, the irater he got. It was obvious that there was no calming him down in this state. I could sense the panic in his eyes that started to arise after he was becoming more and more aware that he had bitten off more than he could chew with this project. He kept repeating, over and over, that he couldn't do it, that he couldn't do it. Panic started to rise within me at this point. I was rapidly becoming aware that the amount of alcohol he consumed that night had such an effect on him and his insecurities. I knew it was a mistake to even consider stopping at the liquor store. I tried urging him to come to bed and that we would discuss it more in the morning, but there was no calming him at this point. He was on another level. I could sense the chaos rising. He ran over to the bathroom, beer in hand, and locked himself in there. I began knocking on the door, trying to persuade him to come out. At this point, he was yelling and blaming me for getting him into this mess. Now I was starting to get angry. This was a joint effort and how could he possibly put the blame on me for not having the confidence in himself to do this project? I didn't force him into anything, and we both agreed this would be a good investment financially in our lives. I started to turn the doorknob and open the door. The lock was busted, and it didn't take much to force the door open. I began pushing on the door with my shoulder and eventually got through. Ben was sitting, hunched over the bathtub ledge, clearly distraught and still yelling at me to get out of the bathroom and leave him alone. I knew he had gone overboard, and I didn't want him to finish his beer because clearly, he had had enough. I tried to pry the beer out of his hands, but he clung on for dear life. He got up, pulled the beer out of my hands, and pushed me out of the bathroom. This was the most aggressive I had ever seen him and the first time he had become physical with me. I didn't understand what had made him get to this point, especially since I had been sleeping for the past few hours. He was an alcoholic left alone for hours to consume a case of beer by himself while left alone with his own thoughts and demons. I was in disbelief at his behavior when I decided to go back to bed, and decided we would address it in the morning. Finally, after tossing and turning after the events I just took part in, I fell back asleep as he finished the last of his beer in the bathroom by himself.

That morning, the confusion quickly came back to me as I started to recall the series of events from the night before. I didn't know where this violent and aggressive behavior had come from, because I had not seen this for the past 10 months that he had been home. It scared me. I knew it had to be the alcohol, but I was still confused because my dad never acted this way when he was drinking to excess. We sat down and had a pretty serious discussion about what had occurred the night before, and Ben was in agreement that it had gotten out of control. He confessed that he was feeling extremely overwhelmed and felt under qualified to be building a home all on his own. It began to become a reality for him when we moved into the house. As we began demolition in the main house for renovations while we waited for permits, he kept convincing himself that he wasn't fit for this project. He hadn't communicated any of this to me. I had no idea he had been feeling this way for weeks on end. I felt nervous and instantly betrayed that he had led me to believe that he could do this, and now he was telling me he couldn't. I didn't know how this would affect our plans for the future and how we would shift our future plans based on this new knowledge.

Once the alcohol started to wear off, however, Ben' confidence began to reappear, and I could sense he was feeling more convinced in his capabilities. He decided that we would take it one step at a time and that he would figure it out on his own. I was hesitant, but I knew I had to trust him if we were planning on getting married the following year. It shook me pretty badly seeing the state he had been in the night before, and I wasn't exactly comfortable coming to an agreement that he would try to better control the alcohol intake the next time. I wasn't sure if I wanted there to be a next time, but this was a time when my friends were all out partying, having the time of their lives, enjoying their 20s, and I wanted to be a part of it too. I had always been part of it and the past eight months' sobriety had taken a toll on my friendships. I hadn't been going out to the bars with them, going for drinks and dinners and meeting new people every weekend. I felt like I had to stay in and support Ben because I knew that he was struggling, and I hadn't recognized the fact that I had been struggling with it all myself. I was so focused on his recovery that I wasn't paying attention to mine. It was almost a bit of a relief that we were going to allow ourselves to loosen up a little bit and live that life that I had been missing out on. My dad was getting away with it still, and so why couldn't we?

We couldn't have admitted it to our families. Ben' parents had been extremely supportive throughout his sobriety and recovery, and we both knew that they would have gone into panic mode if they did find out he was drinking again. We kept it from my mom also, but thought it was safe to share the information with my dad. He was safe for us to confide in him because that meant we could share the enjoyment of our alcohol all together. We began drinking at Dad's on the weekends, and I would go out with my friends once in a while. Ben was extremely jealous and didn't enjoy the fact that I would go out with my girlfriends and meet them at the bars. I can't really blame him though, because I knew I let my drinking get out of hand too. Maybe not to the aggressive level that he had gotten to, but I still got to a point where I no longer had much control over what I was doing or saying throughout the night. One Saturday night, I had met some friends at a pub on the waterfront who I hadn't seen in months. I hadn't been aware that Ben was standing out across from the pub near the boat docks watching me. I knew he was a jealous person, but he was specifically hiding and watching me to find something to accuse me of. When I got home from the pub, he began to accuse me of cheating on him. I had given one of my guy friends a hug after not having seen him for months, and this led Ben into a jealous frenzy. I felt like I had to defend myself for giving someone a very platonic hug. I knew he'd been drinking that night, and this was where his anger was stemming from. I went to bed that night feeling confused and betrayed that he didn't trust me and had to go behind my back and watch me from a distance to find any kind of excuse to accuse me of my behavior.

This cycle of jealousy and insecurity became more and more prevalent as the drinking continued. The anger and outbursts continued and were starting to make me doubt my decision to agree to marry him. It hadn't even been a full year since he had left treatment and we had so many responsibilities on our plates, which didn't help with the stress levels. I didn't feel confident that it was the right decision for me, but when I tried to talk to him about possibly pushing the wedding date, he would get angry. I believed that he was afraid I would leave if he agreed to hold off on the wedding. This was a very distinct time where Ben' abandonment issues were revealing themselves. We had already put a deposit down on the wedding venue and began planning and scheduling with our vendors for the big day. My family and friends could see the stress and strain on our relationship but weren't comfortable bringing it up to me that they thought we should hold off. I didn't want to disappoint anyone, let alone Ben. One weekend, we were at my grandparents' for dinner, and my mom approached me about the wedding. She wanted to let me know that it was OK if I wanted to hold off on the wedding plans because she could sense the turmoil in our relationship. She thought it was too much to take on in such a short period of time, which it was. We were living in a constant state of chaos, and this was yet another piece that was adding to the stress. I knew in my gut that it was the right thing to hold off on the wedding, but I knew if I wanted to go forward with postponing, it would upset Ben. I was already constantly walking on eggshells around him it felt like, and I didn't want to add fire to the flame. This would agitate him, and then who knows how he would have reacted to this change in plans. I wasn't prepared to upset him in the state he was in, and so I convinced my family and myself that I was ready to go ahead with it all and we would work on things together.

Those next couple months were a blur and a whirlwind for me because of everything that was going on in my life. Ben and I were building a home together on very little income, preparing and making plans for our wedding. Not only were we drinking, but we were betraying our families as we continued to drink while my parents were going through their own separation because of my dad's drinking habits and affairs. Ben and I began fighting constantly because we were under an extreme amount of stress, and I knew a large part of it was being contributed by the drinking. I couldn't even blame the excessive drinking on just him because I knew I was drinking in excess at this point to cope with the stress.

It was a vicious cycle that winter. I started to become severely depressed. I would come home from work at the end of a long day to find a lack of progress on the carriage home, or I would come home early from work to find Ben still lying-in bed. We were both feeling the pressure and couldn't avoid the stress we were under and the anticipated arguments. I was working full time to try to carry us financially but was struggling because Ben would constantly be spending unnecessary money that we didn't even have. I couldn't control what he was doing when I was gone to work, but I would find new purchases and lavish meals on the bank statements when I checked online. This was extremely frustrating to me because he had such manic behavior. One minute, he was in frenzy mode because we were so tight for cash that we were worried we wouldn't be able to make the next mortgage payment, and the next day he was avoiding his responsibilities to the house by going to the mall and spending money on impertinent items and clothes. I think back now and wonder if he did suffer from bi-polar tendencies. Not only was he taking multiple medications for his depression and anxiety, but the medication he took was prescribed for antipsychotics, schizophrenia, and bipolar disorder, although he hadn't made me aware if he'd been been diagnosed formally for either.

I began to sink into a slow and deep depression myself. I was so busy taking care of Ben emotionally and financially that I neglected to notice my own feelings of despair. It caught up to me when I began having trouble sleeping at night. I became increasingly exhausted during the day and wired at night. My sleep cycle was totally reversed. I had these endless feelings of doom and despair, and I couldn't talk to Ben about it because he was so emotionally fragile at this point. I needed someone to lean on, and the more that I realized I couldn't lean on him, the more depressed I became. I felt like I was the parent and was in a constant losing battle. It would be after midnight most nights when I couldn't fall asleep. I knew I would have to be up in the morning for work, and I would leave most mornings while Ben continued sleeping in, waking up on his own alarm clock and beginning his day. This was creating some resentment for me while I went to work for the day, and he was building this home leisurely at his own pace. He didn't seem to have any concern that we were on a schedule or that I couldn't continue to carry us forever financially. I would bring it up to him about how I was feeling but he would get immediately defensive, and it would become a major argument. I felt like I was getting nowhere most of the time and I wasn't being heard. This was another contribution to my depression I was falling into. When I couldn't sleep, I would go sit in the kitchen on the countertop and cry to myself. I thought a lot about cutting myself at this point, even to just get some kind of reaction out of him. I began to make little incisions on my wrists, which grew into bigger and deeper incisions. I wanted Ben to notice the slits on my wrists so he could physically see the turmoil and sadness that our life was bringing me. I wanted empathy from him, so he would be able to understand why I was feeling this way and for him to actually hear me rather than get defensive and angry when I confronted him. There was so much chaos and anarchy during that winter that there would have to be some kind of change in order for us to continue. We were in too deep at this point; it was more than just our relationship that was struggling. There were many thoughts that crossed my mind regarding holding off the wedding or stepping away from the relationship altogether, but there were financial gains at stake, and it wasn't just an easy decision to end ties and go our separate ways.

This turmoil inside me led to a conversation about our drinking habits that had formed. I pleaded with Ben to come to an agreement that we would both stop drinking so we could mend the damage that had developed over the past couple months. I believed then, as even now, that alcohol was the major contributor to our disarray. We needed to come back to a healthy place like when he was first out of treatment so we could begin the relationship again from a fresh start. He agreed and knew we couldn't continue on the way it was going. We made a pact and promised each other that we would stay abstinent from alcohol going forward. I absolutely knew this was the right decision and was prepared to abstain from any alcohol at all. It's not like we were drinking every single day, but when we did, it would definitely get out of hand. It wasn't just the immediate effects either; it was the beaten path that would follow us for weeks after. I wasn't even aware of the effects this had on Ben as he mixed alcohol with his medications. It was chemically misbalancing his brain on a neurological and emotional level. One of the medications Ben was prescribed was called Seroquel. It is an anti-psychotic, and it rebalances the concentrations of certain neurotransmitters in the brain. Many doctors advise avoiding alcohol completely when on this type of medication because there can be severe side effects just from it alone. Because Seroquel is used to treat bipolar and schizophrenia patients, when patients mix alcohol with this medication, there can be symptoms such as dizziness, low blood pressure, and motor skills can become impaired. Even thinking and other necessary functions become weakened when mixed together. Ben would constantly forget to take his medication and then double up when he missed a dose, so I couldn't imagine what this was doing to his brain function when mixed with alcohol. He knew the risks associated with mixing the two, and I knew it would be dangerous to continue to drink going forward.

We had made the pact. We would continue to work on our relationship and come to a healthier place together. There would be zero tolerance for slip ups and any more relapses.

Chapter 4

Winter quickly faded into spring and there was rapid progress on the house construction. Finally, after what felt like months, we were finishing up on the final renovations in the main house. We had been living in a construction zone for far too long, but now we were able to get a good head start on the carriage house. The last crumbs of snow were melting steadily, and it was beginning to warm up to springtime temperatures which would make working outdoors more enjoyable for Ben. Within a short amount of time, he was able to pour the foundation, frame the exterior of the house, and it was beginning to look like a home. This was such a relief for me to see the physical progress and momentum. Even though I knew I was still suffering from depression, I was starting to recognize the affect the warm weather and daily sunshine had on my wellbeing. In the Okanagan, the winters are known for their overcast skies and dreary weather, so it's not uncommon to hear of someone experiencing the winter blues.

We were still working on prioritizing our finances while I was working full time trying to support us. I had begun working with a real estate team who were a couple, and I was doing administration support in their home office. It wasn't my dream job by any means, but I enjoyed the work and the woman I worked for. Her husband, however, was not my cup of tea. He was extremely inappropriate with me, and I felt uncomfortable each time we would be in the office together alone. When we were alone, he would confide in me about sexual occurrences in his marriage, and I wouldn't even begin to understand why he would tell me this kind of information. There would be occasions where he would make sexual comments and innuendos toward me that would make my skin crawl. Each morning I showed up for work, I would pray that his vehicle wouldn't be in the driveway, and he would be away for business or out for a showing appointment. I watched as he treated his wife the same way. His wife, who I came to really admire, was one of the hardest working women I knew. When she wasn't out selling property, she was working relentlessly in her office, making phone calls and setting up appointments. I didn't understand why she was still married to this guy because he treated her with such disrespect right in front of me all the time. I barely saw him ever doing real work and he would travel down to the Caribbean frequently, claiming that he was doing business down there. He couldn't have been doing much real estate in the Tropics because I never actually saw any transactions happening through the business.

It was April, just a month and a half before our wedding date and were just gaining momentum with the carriage house when I showed up to work one morning as usual, put my lunch in the fridge, and then made myself a coffee. I hadn't gotten one sip down before I had to run upstairs to the bathroom to vomit. This wave of nausea came flooding over me by surprise. I felt fine that morning while I was getting ready for work, but all of a sudden, I could barely even stand. I felt weak and lightheaded. I thought I must have caught a bug. I continued about my day and went home feeling better than I had that morning. The next morning, the same wave of nausea crept up on me again as I ran to the bathroom for a second time. When I finished, I began to put the pieces together and instantly realized that I was late on my period. *I couldn't be pregnant,* I thought. There was absolutely no way that we were in a position to begin planning for a baby as we were just months away from getting married and then would be selling the house. My head started spinning as I thought of all the different occurrences and slip-ups that could have happened in the past month in order for me to get pregnant. I was normally so careful and adamant, with my birth control pills, but during the past couple months, my mind was focused on so many other things that sometimes I would miss a pill but wouldn't think too much about it. I knew I had forgotten to take them a couple days those past few weeks, but my naïve understanding was that he pills would still be in your system to protect against unwanted pregnancy. I called Ben immediately that morning once I realized my situation, and he immediately went out to get a pregnancy test. I wanted to have it there when I returned home from work that evening, while the two of us would be together to find out. I could barely concentrate at work that day, and when it was finally time to leave, I rushed home to find the pregnancy test sitting overtly on the counter. We had both been waiting anxiously all day to take the test and find out the results.

I peed on the stick, and it didn't take long for the second line to start showing a positive result. I read the directions, and the test said that you needed to wait at least three minutes for the results, but it was clear by the immediate result that I was indeed pregnant. It made sense.

All the ups and downs of emotions that I have been feeling recently, the missed period, and the nausea and vomiting. I didn't know how to feel. I showed the results to Ben, and I could tell that he wasn't excited about the news. I knew he wouldn't be overjoyed at the fact that I was pregnant, but I wasn't prepared for his extreme reaction to it. He was clearly upset. I examined him as he withdrew immediately and was not the support that I needed him to be when finding out that I was pregnant. He instantly assumed that we would have an abortion and that would take care of it. I wasn't allowed to have my opinion on the matter. Even if I had felt a little excited at the thought of being a parent, there was just no discussing another option. After trying to express how I was feeling, he finally gave me an ultimatum. It was either him or the baby. He said he would not be around to support us if I did decide to go ahead with the pregnancy. This was such a shock to me because I was emotionally raw at the news of finding out I was pregnant, and then my husband-to-be, who I was about to marry in a month's time, was telling me I had to abort the baby if I wanted to get married. I knew there was no way that I could raise this baby on my own. I was an emotional wreck and it scared me to know that he could shut himself off so easily from such a life changing decision. A decision that wasn't only his to make. The reason he gave me was that he wasn't prepared or willing to bring a child into the world who would potentially struggle with mental health and addiction issues like his or her parents. Back then, I knew we weren't stable and financially set to raise a child, but we had family who would support us in whichever decision we made. He was just so convincing when he wanted something, and there was no changing his mind.

Those next few days, I knew I would have to make one of the hardest decisions of my life. Because I had only just taken one at home pregnancy test, I would have to go to the doctor and officially confirm the pregnancy before sharing the news with my family. That week, when I went to see the doctor, we booked my first ultrasound, and from there we would schedule the abortion. The procedure had to be performed within a certain amount of time because the doctors wouldn't perform the abortion after a certain number of weeks. It took a few weeks to get in for the procedure, so I had to book it in and secure a spot so I wouldn't go over the 12-week time frame, after which they wouldn't be able to perform it. It didn't leave much time for backing out because I was already 6 weeks into my first trimester.

I knew that the ultimatum stemmed from Ben's insecurities around him being adopted. He explained to me that between the two of our genetic backgrounds, our child would either end up an addict, with mental health issues, or both. He was afraid to bring a child into this world without much chance of a normal life. I, however, didn't agree with this. I knew that one day I would be a good mother who would care for my child unconditionally and that it wasn't a fair choice that he had given me.

I went to my mom and told her about our situation. I knew I could trust my family with this news, but I was afraid to bring it up to my in-laws until we knew what we were going to do. My mom was supportive, although she did persuade me to look at other options. My sisters felt the same way. They were supportive but also wanted me to look into other options so this baby would have a chance at life. I explained to them the situation that Ben had put me in, and the decision I had to make. I knew it was my body and ultimately my decision, but our relationship was so fragile as we were getting back on track with a sober lifestyle that I didn't want to do anything that might send our progress backward.

It was a heavy-hearted couple of days. As I waited to hear the official date from my doctor, Ben and I had a very uneasy time awaiting the date for abortion. I was a complete emotional wreck and I felt like I was lying to everyone, including myself. One night that week, we went to his parents for dinner like we usually did every week or two, and I showed up early, as I had finished my day earlier than expected. I had always felt very comfortable with his parents. They were extremely caring and supportive of our relationship, although I always felt like they believed we rushed into things too quickly. We were visiting as Ben pulled up in the driveway in his truck and came into the house. I went to kiss him and say hello, and as soon as I pulled away from him, my stomach sank, and I knew that he had been drinking. I could smell it on him immediately. It scared me because all those anxious feelings came rushing back to me from the first night that he had drank after over a full year of sobriety. I couldn't hide the fact that he smelled like booze from his parents, so I dragged him down the stairs to talk to him in private. I was furious but shocked at the same time. I was in disbelief that he would drink during this emotional time. I asked him pointedly if he had been drinking, and he lied to me on the spot. He told me he went for what he called "near beer" and had a couple non-alcoholic beers, which is why he smelled like it. I could tell by his behavior that he was lying. How could he show up at his parents, emanating like beer and not expect them to know. Everything was still a secret with them, and we hadn't admitted the relapse or the struggles we'd been having with the pregnancy. At this point, I was so tempted to admit the whole predicament to them because I knew how loving they were and how much support they would have given us. I didn't feel like I had any support from Ben and that I was on my own with everything. I wouldn't let up on him and prodded him for the truth. Eventually, after I relentlessly hounded him, he did admit that he had had a few beers, and that it wasn't a big deal every once in a while. I was completely devastated by him telling me this. I had been completely sober after our discussion that there would be zero alcohol tolerance going forward, and he had betrayed me.

He betrayed my trust, and this was just another instance that showed me he wasn't ready or serious about staying sober. I broke down and began to sob uncontrollably. His parents heard me and came rushing down to find out what was going on, but Ben begged me to stay quiet. I wanted so badly to open up to them about the fact that he was drinking behind my back and that I was pregnant. I was in desperate need of some of their support. I couldn't even look at them. I was so ashamed that we had been lying for months and all they were trying to do was to love us. They wanted the best for us. I felt so guilty that when I needed them the most, I couldn't even be honest with them about anything that was really going on. I had to think of something quick, so I told them a lie about feeling overwhelmed with wedding plans and the emotional distress that my parents' divorce was causing me. I knew both of those were true to some extent, but I could not divulge the entire truth. I was afraid of what Ben would have done or said after we'd left. He was so unstable, and I felt like I was walking on eggshells since I got the pregnancy news, and I wasn't sure what would happen if I told his parents the truth.

We left that evening in our separate cars and decided that we would discuss it more at home. When we got home, Ben admitted that he was feeling pressure and stress and needed something to relieve it. I had been feeling the same pressure and stress, but I knew what kind of path it would lead if we both started drinking again. I pleaded with him that we had to be completely sober and that we would have to rely on each other when we were struggling. He agreed, and said he was sorry for the slip up. I wanted to believe that that would be the last time that would happen, but I knew it was a long road ahead.

As the wedding date crept closer and closer, there were so many emotional highs and lows. I had decided to go forward with getting an abortion because I knew that I was not ready to raise a baby on my own. I couldn't have trusted Ben to stay if I had gone ahead with the pregnancy, and I knew I couldn't have lived with the thought of giving up my child to anyone else. It wasn't an easy decision, but I felt confident that I had made the right choice for me and for my marriage. I had learned at an early age to shut down my emotions, and this was just another instance that I would have to do it again. I was so young, and I knew there would be plenty of time ahead to try for a family in the future. I went ahead and booked the procedure for about a week after our wedding day. I would be just before the 12-week mark, and that was the latest I could push it, just in case I did change my mind. My mom wasn't happy, but she knew the reasons behind my decision.

As wedding plans got underway, I began to feel even less confident about our future together. Ben was sticking to his promise to stay sober, but the way we were dealing with our issues was not getting any better. He still wasn't consistent with his medications, and I knew that was half the battle. We were fighting constantly over finances and the progress of the house. The idea of us having a happy, healthy marriage into our older years began to fade for me. The fantasy of growing old with my soul mate was slowly slipping through my fingers, and it felt like a facade. I hoped my feelings would change eventually back to how I felt when he got out of treatment. I couldn't change course now, though, and disappoint my family, friends, and Ben.

May quickly arrived, and it was just weeks until my wedding day. My girlfriends had organized a dinner out as a substitute for a bachelorette party. They knew I wanted something low key, so we agreed to meet at a restaurant for dinner. When I got there, they were all drinking cocktails, and I knew it wouldn't be an uneasy conversation to explain to them that I wasn't drinking again. I knew it would have been confusing to them because just months ago, we were all drinking and partying together like nothing had changed. I explained the situation about how we were working on being sober again and that in order for me to support Ben – that meant that I couldn't drink either. They were annoyed and wanted to give me a bachelorette party as one "last hurrah" before I tied the knot. They saw it as Ben's addiction, not mine, and I shouldn't have to change my lifestyle habits for him. They kept urging me to have just one drink and that Ben wouldn't mind because it was my "bachelorette" party. They just didn't understand what kind of effect one drink would have on our marriage at this point. I refused, and I could see the disappointment on their faces. They had always known me as the party girl who would easily take down multiple shots in a row and wouldn't hesitate to take a free drink from anyone. It was a new me, but I knew the consequences it would cause if I had taken that drink. I wanted to be a strong support system for Ben even though I would have enjoyed having a few that night with my girls but I didn't like the fact that my best friends weren't being supportive of me. Looking back now, I know they were confused at the fact that one week we would be drinking and partying at my dad's and then the next, Ben and I were back to being sober. They weren't safe for me to come and talk to back then. I was afraid of having to hold myself accountable for our actions. I knew they were confused, but I just didn't have the energy or capacity to divulge everything to them because I was so emotionally burned out myself. Finally, they did back off and didn't hound me to have a drink after a while, and we discussed wedding plans and honeymoon plans.

I always had a sense that Ben wouldn't grow old with me. For some reason, I had a gut instinct that he would die young. I can't explain my intuition on this, but it was just a feeling I couldn't shake. It was terrible of me to think that back then, but I knew that getting married to the love of his life was something that he always wanted. He would tell me that he dreamed about the day he would walk down the aisle to meet his soul mate and profess his vows. He was such a hopeless romantic, and part of me felt that I would be robbing him of this if I didn't follow through. I knew he was my soul mate and I wanted to marry my best friend, but I was constantly fighting the feeling that it just wasn't the right time. I was also struggling with the fact that we had recently uncovered the cheating scandals that my mom had discovered in my dad's journal. I think that this information affected me more than I had even realized. Just months before getting married to Ben, I found out that my dad, whom I trusted unconditionally and wouldn't have thought could have done any sort of things like this, had completely destroyed my trust in family and marriage. If he could betray my mom so easily and for so long, what were the chances Ben could? Ben was still working at gaining my trust back, and we had a long way to go. If he could drink behind my back, why couldn't he cheat also? I began to see a therapist once a week to try and gain some clarity about my emotions and hesitations around the wedding. I wasn't completely honest with her about everything, but it felt good to get some things off my chest that had been bothering me. Eventually, after a few sessions, she gave me the go ahead and told me she thought I was ready. I knew she didn't know the whole story and I knew I was only cheating myself by not being completely transparent. I should have known it would take more than just a few sessions to gain her trust and divulge all the personal details of our relationship I was so fragile with trust at this point, I didn't have much assurance in anything or anyone. I don't really know why I even bothered to go in the first place, because I just wasn't ready to fully admit how I was feeling to anyone, including myself.

Chapter 5

It was May 2008, and I had taken the week off prior to the wedding to tie up loose ends and finalize last minute details. Ben didn't have anything planned for his bachelor party, so him and his brother planned to drive three hours from Kelowna to the coast to skydive together. They organized this event for the day before our wedding. This made me nervous because I had never done anything like skydiving before, but Ben was such an adrenaline junkie that it really didn't surprise me that that was what he wanted to do.

That week, I took care of loose ends like the music playlists, picking up the flowers, seating charts, and a few other miscellaneous tasks. The night before the wedding, I stayed at my mom's, and after Ben and his brother got back from their skydiving adventure, they stayed with their parents. While staying at my mom's, I was feeling all sorts of emotions. My mom could sense that I was a little on edge, and she pulled me aside to let me know that if I didn't want to go through with it, I still had time. I knew she wanted me to be happy, but she also wanted me to make the right decision. She was being supportive and wanted to let me know that I shouldn't feel forced into doing it if I was feeling any kind of hesitation. I lied and told her I was ready. Even though I was just about three months pregnant and heading into my second trimester, I felt confident that even though I wasn't one hundred percent ready, I wasn't prepared to call it all off. I think part of me felt I had to keep convincing myself at this point that we were making the right decisions because it was scarier for me to think of what would happen if we didn't get married and I did continue on with the pregnancy. I had to trust the process even though I didn't know exactly where it would lead me.

May 25th was the morning of the wedding, and I woke up and the house was busy. My three sisters were my bridesmaids, and we had scheduled a friend who was a hair stylist to come do each of our hair and makeup. It was such a blur of a morning with all the activity going on. Once we were ready, the photographers arrived and began taking snapshots of the pre-wedding activity. I wore a beautiful strapless wedding dress that hugged my hips and had a long train at the back with a bow. I paired it with my mom's pearl earrings that she lent me for the day and a rhinestone bracelet. It was simple but timeless. My hair was half pulled back and curled in just the right places. I felt beautiful. My older sister told me I was the most gorgeous bride she had ever seen, and I felt it. It was all coming together, and in those few hours, it felt right.

The limo arrived and we got a few more photos before my sisters and I climbed in to begin our drive together to the venue. When my sisters popped open a bottle of champagne, I felt a pang of resentment and regret that I couldn't join in on my wedding day. I settled for some sparkling juice as an alternative. They told me that I could have just a sip and they wouldn't tell, but I knew if Ben smelled any lingering of alcohol on me, it could be disastrous. Especially while we were saying our vows, I didn't know how he would react if he knew. It scared me too much, so I swigged down the nonalcoholic beverage that I was provided instead. We arrived at the venue and immediately got out of the limo to go to a private room where we took more family photos before the ceremony commenced.

It was an elegant location for a wedding. The venue was situated on an 18-hole golf course, which overlooked the city and the lake. The ceremony and reception were all held outside, underneath a tent lit up with string lights. Behind the altar, there was a quiet waterfall cascading from a pond with a beautiful red bridge crossing over it. Beautiful full brush and flowers surrounded the water feature, and it looked exactly like what we had expected. We didn't require much more foliage as it was rich in itself.

It had rained that morning, but the sun was just starting to come out as the ceremony was about to begin. The clouds began to part, and the sun shone through as the music started. The scene was out of a fairytale. Ben and his groomsman headed toward the ceremony area as the DJ cranked Metallica – Enter Sandman. They were all dressed in black suits, wearing black matching sunglasses. It was just like Ben to request to enter his wedding ceremony wearing sunglasses and marching to a rock song. It definitely created a different vibe than what I'd known traditional weddings to be.

Once they were all at the altar, I got the cue that the bridesmaids were ready to enter down the long path toward the stand, and they began to enter one by one. Finally, as I crept behind them without being seen, I could hear the DJ switch to my entrance song, and I knew it was time. I could hear the violins on the speakers and began my way toward the aisle. I couldn't think of anything other than making it to the altar without my knees buckling out of nervousness. My dad walked with me, and I could feel the eyes of our eighty guests' on me as I made my entrance to the music.

I had chosen a beautiful instrumental with violins and piano from one of my favorite movie soundtracks. It was a movie I had watched in theaters while Ben was in rehab, and the movie really resonated with me. The main actor reminded me of Ben, and I felt like it was a sign that we would be together when he got home. It was a movie that I connected with on an emotional level, and the music gave me a feeling of hope. I continued down the aisle as the instrumentals picked up pace, reached the altar and hugged my dad. I met my future husband face-to-face as we stood in front of each other. I could feel my hands shaking uncontrollably. I don't know if it was the nerves of being in front of eighty people about to confess my love and commitment to this person for the rest of my life or if I was having hesitations and was too afraid to back out. There were too many things running through my mind and not enough time to think logically.

The ceremony was brief as we repeated after the justice of the peace and signed our marriage certificates. I felt relieved that it was over and that there was no going back. It was only going forward now. Ben seemed the happiest I'd seen him in a long time as we linked arms and made our way to the front lobby of the clubhouse to take some photos.

The rest of the day sailed on smoothly, even when the rain began to pour later in the evening. We had a delicious dinner followed by dancing and games that the DJ entertained us with. Even though it was a dry wedding, we kept hearing comments from guests that it was one of the most entertaining weddings they had attended. This relieved me as many of our guests would likely be anticipating some kind of bar. I had given my friends a warning that there wouldn't be any alcohol; however, they still brought their own to the reception and hid it. To my surprise, they were passing around a bottle of vodka under the table secretively, which only made me feel like I wasn't being supported 100% even more. They weren't supporting me or my marriage, and I felt this way with my dad, as I knew he was also drinking during the reception. I felt hurt, but it was more proof for me that I would have to distance myself from my friends if I wanted to continue to support Ben's sobriety and get back to a place where we weren't constantly on edge.

Our guests began to leave around ten o'clock that night, and we were ready to leave and go to our bed and breakfast that we had booked for the wedding night. We booked a Mediterranean-style bed and breakfast in a guest suite that overlooked the lake and mountains. It was secluded and private, and the perfect place to relax after a long day. We had a private hot tub on the patio, which we immediately took advantage of once we checked in and then went inside and fell asleep in our bathrobes.

The next day, my mom hosted an open house type lunch where we would open gifts and visit one last time with family and guests that had come from out of town. I still felt awkward because no one in Ben's family knew I was pregnant, and being almost twelve weeks along, I was beginning to show. I knew it was noticeable and I had to start wearing loose-fitting shirts so I wouldn't give my secret away. I had wondered if people had noticed my bump in my wedding dress the day prior, but no one had mentioned anything to me.

Ben and I planned to spend our honeymoon hidden away at a private campground where we could fish, hike, and relax, just the two of us, for three days in the mountains. This was our idea of a perfect time spent away together, so that next week we packed up our tent, sleeping bags, and camp gear and began the drive up the mountain to a quiet campground that we knew would be the perfect place to connect. I had booked off that week specifically so we could take a honeymoon camping trip before I had to go in for my abortion procedure. It was early June, but the campground was quiet as it was mid-week and had a lake filled with trout and pike. We had borrowed a fishing boat and rods from Ben's aunt so we could try to catch our evening dinner. I began to love fishing since I was with Ben because it was such a peaceful way to spend time together in the middle of the lake where there were no noises or distractions. It was a time I cherished with him because he was in his element in nature and it was an easy way to connect, which we did that honeymoon week.

That next week after returning home, I returned to work where I uneasily anticipated the coming days ahead. After all the excitement and distraction of the wedding, I hadn't had much time to process the abortion that would be coming up within a few days. I had it scheduled for a Tuesday, so I had only a few days to prepare myself, which I really didn't even know how to do. I was so consumed the last couple months with the wedding and now this uncertain termination was becoming a reality that I hadn't fully emotionally prepared myself for. I didn't know what to expect other than what my doctor had briefly told me. I didn't even book the day off work because I had taken off two weeks' prior for the wedding and honeymoon and I was definitely not about to explain why I needed a day off to my employers. This was information I wasn't even willing to share with certain family members, so I would have to bite the bullet and push through it.

Ben drove me to work that Tuesday, as my appointment wasn't scheduled until the later morning. I told my boss I would come in to do some work in the morning first thing and then leave for an appointment I had scheduled, which may take a couple hours and return back to finish the day. I was at the hospital around eleven o'clock that morning, and as we pulled up, I could see all the protestors outside with their signs and anti-abortion shirts. This was a common weekly occurrence. They showed up once a week on Tuesdays, flashing their signs to discourage mothers for going through with the abortion. I passed the hospital to work each morning and noticed this more often since finding out that I was pregnant months ago, and it was disconcerting to me as we pulled into the parking lot. The hospital visit was brief. We checked in. The nurses gave me a gown to dress in and pills for the pain. I wasn't expecting much pain, as I had read that it wasn't always that painful. We went into the room where the doctor greeted us. She made me feel extremely comfortable and I felt like I was making the right decision. She made me feel like it was OK to be terminating my pregnancy, but for me, it was such a strange experience. She seemed confident that everything would go smoothly, and I began to relax a little. I hadn't always been comfortable with hospitals, as I usually associated them with death and illness. I was already on edge with multiple unknowns; the biggest unknown being not knowing how I'd feel after terminating my unborn fetus and not feeling like I had much of a choice.

The doctor told me to lie back in the chair with my legs up and spread out on individual stirrups. She asked if I wanted any sedation medication, but I knew I had to return to work after this, and didn't want anything that might make me groggy, as I knew I wouldn't be able to perform my work the rest of the afternoon. I figured the ibuprofen and Advil that I took would be plenty. She began to enter me with a vacuum-type suction hose, and I could immediately feel the pain in my uterus area. The cramping was excruciating. I had only lasted thirty seconds or so when I could not go on further without any sedation. I explained that I had to go back to work, so they did a minimal amount that would suffice until the procedure was over. I wasn't expecting this kind of pain. The sedation helped a little, but the cramps that were to come later on were the ones that would nearly kill me. It was about 10 minutes before it was all over, and they had me lie in a bed until the sedation wore off and to monitor me before they released me. Ben stayed with me the entire time, and I felt numb afterward. I could tell that he felt relieved. I was saddened by this but still fairly groggy from the pain and medications to really talk about it. After a half hour, they released me after feeding me crackers and juice and informed me that it would still be a two-to-three-day recovery period as there would be bleeding, then light spotting and cramping. Once I was release, Ben drove me back to work, and I was relieved to find there was no one in the office. I don't know how I thought I could return to work given the emotional and physical state I was in.

That afternoon, I tried to get a bit of work done, but I couldn't focus, and the cramping was too unbearable to even sit in an upright position. Luckily, there was a sofa in the next room where I could lie down and suffer through the stabs of cramps that came every few minutes. I felt like maybe this is what labor felt like.

I finished off the rest of the day and was relieved to go home and lie on the couch for the rest of the evening. I knew Ben sympathized with me, but he couldn't have physically or emotionally felt what I had just gone through. I continued to bleed for a few days after that, and by the weekend I was starting to feel better. I must have been in serious denial because we had gone ahead with the wedding and taken care of the abortion within a matter of weeks, and now I felt we could move forward and not dwell on the past. There was still plenty to look forward to with finishing the house, selling, and beginning a new project that fall. We would make it through the summer by finishing up the last details, listing the property in the fall and putting the angst and stress behind us. We only had a few more months to get through as it was already June, and we could potentially list in September. This was our aspiration for a brighter and successful future that hopefully would go according to plan.

Looking back now, there was so much going on in our lives that I couldn't have possibly begun to process each step and milestone that we had gone through up until this point. Whenever we thought we were getting through one obstacle, there was another one right up against us to battle.

I had once again learned to shut down my emotions because I was so consumed with the chaos that was going on in our lives that I managed to turn everything off mentally and to just make it through each day. There was such a lack of stability that it was a scary thought to commit to making a change with the way things were going because I felt like my life was so out of control. Whether it was struggling with finances, sobriety, or any surprises that life was throwing our way we continued to power through and try to rely on each other to make the necessary changes that were needed. The problem was that neither of us were making any of those necessary changes that were vital to our sobriety, finances and most of all, mental health.

Chapter 6

Summer 2008 went by in a flash. Our entire focus was on final details for the completion of the house. If I wasn't working my regular day job, I was helping Ben with the finishing touches at the carriage house. That summer, I learned how to cut and install tile, install kitchen cabinets, and I even tackled laying shingles on the roof. It was just about time to list the property after we finished the last part of our project, landscaping. Once it was completed, we could finally breathe again. After too many months of living paycheck to paycheck, we would finally be able to start bringing in two sets of income. We hadn't foreseen the amount of time that it would take for completion, but we knew we could list the property, and with the way the housing market was in Kelowna, it wouldn't be long before we were reaping the benefits. Another relief I was looking forward to was knowing that we could live in the carriage home and rent out the main house that we had been living in for nearly a year. We felt ready to make the transition and packed up the entire house and moved thirty feet behind us into the carriage home at the back of the property. It was a quick move, just a few steps through the back yard, and we'd live there until it sold. This would be a big help for us financially, and we planned to sell the property with the main house rented, as this would be an ideal situation for any investor seeking an investment property. Our tenants would just have to put up with showings until it did sell, which we anticipated wouldn't take long anyway.

It was only a couple weeks into the listing when the stock market crashed in the fall of 2008. As the U.S. stock exchange plummeted, so did most investments, which in turn led to a downfall in housing prices. Kelowna's housing market was hit hard by this, and investors were not so willing to buy rental properties or investment opportunities as the interest rates skyrocketed. This situation posed an immediate problem for us, as we had purchased the house at a premium while prices were at an all-time high. In 2007 when we bought, many investors were taking advantage of the profit they could make by buying and flipping homes, which in turn created an inflated market. We bought high, and now were anticipating a low profit margin due to the decrease in pricing we were seeing. We decided to keep it on the market regardless, in case there would be an offer we could settle on. We had to reevaluate our situation and decided it was best if Ben found a job and I found an additional part-time evening job. After needing to constantly borrow money from my dad, who funded this whole project, we were in the red until we could come up with some money to repay him, plus the interest we had agreed on. I could sense Ben's disappointment that there wouldn't be a next project immediately after selling this one and he would have to go work for someone else. He did best when he worked on his own and at his own pace, which sometimes had been at a leisurely speed. He always struggled to keep jobs in the past, and I was a little worried as to how he would be working for a company again.

He began handing out resumes and got hired at a construction company fairly quickly. The project he would be working on was right in the core of downtown, about five blocks away from our house. It was convenient being so close to our home.

I was still working as an assistant to the real estate team, but it was getting slower and slower due to the housing market, and I knew it was another reason I'd have to pick up another part-time gig. My sister was working at a women's shelter which housed women with addictions, and mental health issues who were in transition from abusive relationships or off the streets. I knew it paid well and they were looking for a part-time overnight case worker. I had no experience in this type of work before, but I figured with my experience around addictions in my family, it might be a good opportunity for me to learn a few things and I'd do well. I didn't hesitate to hand in my resume and got a call right away for an interview. Within five minutes of leaving my interview, I had been offered and accepted a new job as an overnight caseworker. The pay started off well above the minimum wage, and I was excited to begin a new endeavor. I would have to work out the details with my other position as it was a day job, but I was confident I could perform at both jobs for the time being.

Ben began working steadily at his construction job, full time, even though it wasn't something he was too crazy about. I was constantly worried with all the complaining he was doing that he was going to do something drastic, like quit or get fired. It was just his character to walk off a job site without thinking it through. I had been so relieved that there was finally an additional income coming in, and I didn't like feeling on edge that he might do something to sever that. He also didn't like the fact that I was gone more in the evenings, even though we didn't really have much of a choice. He began to drive me to work on the weekends, which I thought was sweet of him, but I hadn't realized he had ulterior motives for dropping me off himself. On Friday and Saturday nights that I was scheduled for my eleven o'clock shift, he would drop me off and then go park across the street, watching the shelter I was working in. He was so paranoid that he believed I was pretending to go to work but was sneaking out with my friends to go party. The thought of planning such a charade had never even crossed my mind, and I was surprised he even considered I would do something like that. The paranoia was becoming more and more evident as the weeks went by. I slowly began to wonder if he was drinking again because he had many opportunities now that I was working the graveyard shifts at the women's shelter. I didn't think he would be drinking behind my back while I was working to support us around the clock, and typically after a nine-hour shift through the night, I wouldn't have noticed unless I had proof of bottles lying around or the smell of it on him in the morning. Mostly through the week, he would be gone to work before I could get home to check. I was also so emotionally drained by a nine-hour shift dealing with the women coming in high, or drunk, or sneaking their drugs and paraphernalia into the shelter. As I look back on those days, I wonder what led me to a job working in such chaos when I was living it daily. What made me decide I wanted to submerge myself in a similar environment that I was suffering so much anxiety from.

One night while working at the shelter around two in the morning, there was a woman who was scheduled to get dropped off by the police, and I had to admit her and do her intake. This process generally included taking notes and reporting her history of abuse and noting mental and physical conditions. Then, we would have to search her belongings and go through any medications she might be taking or needing. I was on edge that night because I knew a little bit about her background. She was being brought in after the police had found her in the woods on the side of the highway where a local gang had left her. I assumed it had to do with drugs, but a lot of women in the shelter were sex trade workers, and you never knew what they owed to the gangs or the situations they got into. These gang members had taken her, undressed her, and poured acid on her from her head to her toes.

She came in that night, afraid, and I tried my best to comfort her. I took her to the donation shed where she picked out some clothing and she thanked me for my graciousness. She wrote a poem for me that night and told me she would write another one for me the next day, but when I got to work the next day she had been discharged. She left on her own terms, and I hadn't heard from her again. She touched me that night as she had appreciated my kindness and had written me a personal poem. I took that poem home with me and kept it.

There were so many women from all different walks of life at the shelter. Some of them made me on edge. One girl, who was around my age and whom I really thought sweetly of, was in and out of the shelter often. The most recent time she was there, she was hiding from the same gang as the girl with the acid, and they'd kept her in captivity for thirty days. They had forced her into the sex trade and fed her heroin as bait. She eventually escaped and came to hide at the shelter. I was constantly uneasy, as I never knew who would show up at the shelter looking for these women. We made sure we had every door locked on constant and had security cameras surrounding the property. One Halloween night that fall, around two in the morning there were about ten clients of the home and me with another case worker standing on the back porch taking in some fresh air and smoking cigarettes. Suddenly, we heard a gunshot and footsteps running through the back alley that the shelter backed onto. We knew the shooter was close by, and immediately scrambled back inside to lock the door behind us. We got inside and saw a man being chased by another man with a gun, shooting at him right in front of us. It was one of the most terrifying moments in my life where I was petrified to my core. We got inside, and I couldn't stop shaking and shivering. The police came by shortly to take testimonials from us witnesses, and by the end of the night, I was so drained but shaken up from the whole scenario that I couldn't even fall asleep that morning. I hadn't even been there a full month and I was already afraid to go back for more night shifts.

I had always been terrified of guns, but one of my main fears I'd had was related to Ben's past history in which some of the things he had done previous to me could always come back to haunt us. I worried that at any time, someone could come knocking on our door looking for Ben or I for revenge or payback.

When Ben got out of treatment, he confessed to me some of the criminal activity that he had taken part in prior to his sobriety. One situation he found himself in was when he and two other friends were just outside of town at a secluded beach that was tucked away from tourists and even residents. Most people weren't even aware of this location. I don't even know how, but Ben and his friends found out there would be a large sum of money stowed away in a toolbox in a marked location for a specific drug deal that day. I don't know who could have possibly given him this tip, but the boys tracked down this toolbox stashed of cash and took off with it before anyone could catch them and split the money three ways. This happened before I even knew him, but he was always afraid of being caught later, and from what I saw, I was not in denial about what I thought any gang could be capable of if they were to ever come after us.

I had been working at the shelter for just over a month when I came home one afternoon to find Ben acting strangely. I had gotten a day shift that weekend, and Ben didn't generally work weekends, so he had planned to go fishing with one of his best friends, Corey. They were close friends from college and spent a good amount of time together. My shift ended at 3 pm and I got home close to dinner time, and as I walked in the door, Ben cornered me up against the wall and I could smell alcohol on his breath once again. He was trying to be playful, but I knew there was something off about the whole situation. I was backed up against the wall before I could get a chance to take off my shoes when he told me that he had had near beers and was in a good mood. I felt this was hard to believe and I knew deep down that it wasn't true. I could tell by the way he was acting that there was more to the story. I questioned him over and over, and he began to get frustrated with me when I wouldn't stop the questioning. He assured me that he hadn't consumed any alcoholic beer while he was with Corey on the boat fishing that day and that was that. I couldn't shake the feeling that he possibly could have been drinking again behind my back, and I once again didn't see it coming. I knew I probably should have though because things were not the easiest in our lives at that time and we were both looking for relief when we could get some. Ben was back at work in a job that he didn't overly enjoy. I was working nights and days, and we didn't get to spend a lot of time together, which meant he was on his own most weekend nights and days. We had also just recently put our Rottweiler, Koda, down because she suffered from epilepsy. She would become extremely aggressive after one of her multiple seizures she had each day, and she had bitten the mailman who was riding his bike in front of our house delivering the post. We buried her in our newly landscaped back yard where we thought we would always remember her. Although Ben was managing to stay sober, or so, I thought, he also wasn't attending many AA meetings, which he should have been diligent with because it was only a matter of time before he would start drinking again. He was adamant this time that he could control it. I was so tired of trying to fight him on this repeatedly, so I reluctantly agreed we would have the occasional drink and monitor it in case it got out of control again.

That winter got out of control. Dad was now living at a house on the other side of town and every weekend it seemed like we were there partying. I can't even admit to being the responsible one during this time because Ben and I were both drinking heavily through this period. It was late October, and my sister Maddy's birthday party was held at my dad's house one weekend. There were about 40 friends crammed into my dad's house. It was a good size and could accommodate this many people, but random others began to show up that hadn't been invited. It was starting to get out of control because they were coming in from different entrances around the house. My sister wasn't allowing a certain group of girls that were trying to join the party, and one of the girls ended up punching my sister in the face, leaving her with a sweltering black eye. Ben immediately searched the house for a baseball bat and started to go after the group of girls that had just attacked Maddy. He scrambled for his shoes and took off, fully prepared to knock them out, but by the time he had found the bat and his shoes, they had already taken off. This was the kind of person Ben was. He had no hesitation when it came to protecting his family and getting into any sort of altercation. He lived off of extreme situations and wasn't afraid to jump in to defend no matter what the cost.

Our lives began to spiral when Ben decided one afternoon in November to not go back to his job. He was home for lunch, and he had been complaining daily about the lack of motivation he had for the type of job he was doing. He felt he was more skilled than what his position entailed. I think the reason he was disinterested in his job was that he had just completed building an entire home from the foundation up, and he clearly had more experience than hammering nails into some frame boards that was his position now. He felt he wasn't getting anywhere even though he hadn't been at his job for even three months. It was midweek and a quiet afternoon, so I finished work early to go meet him at home for lunch. After we ate, I figured it was time for him to start making his way back when he told me he wasn't going back for the day. He said he was done. He wanted to find something different and would begin looking right away. I didn't like this idea and pleaded with him to find a job first and then quit, so he had something lined up at least. But he didn't agree. He had always been a risk taker, and this was no different. He wasn't thinking about our future and how this would set us back, he always acted in the now without thinking of consequences. This was very stressful for me as I had just given my notice at the women's shelter because of the long nights and days that I was working between the two jobs and how it was affecting not only my mental state but our marriage. Ben still was questioning me as I went in for the graveyard shifts and I was always anxious to what I was going to come home to in the morning or even afternoon. Now we would be going back to square one because the house still wasn't getting any action and we would be living off of one income again. I couldn't convince him otherwise, so I prayed that he would spend his time off looking for something right away.

It isn't an easy task for someone to gain employment when they aren't actively looking. Within a few weeks of Ben being unemployed, his motivation was quickly diminishing. He began to sleep more and more and began to wean off his medications completely. I knew his depression was beginning to take its toll, and I knew this routine all too well. Once the depression hit, when he would need his meds more than ever, he would begin to conveniently forget to take them, which would send him into a deeper depression and state of mental anguish. It was a vicious cycle when he would attempt this. He would wean off his pills or sometimes quit cold turkey, and his symptoms would begin all over again in a more chaotic position than the last. I would have to convince him that he needed to continue them in order to keep himself balanced neurologically and to feel sane. Mixing this pattern with his drinking, he began to spiral. He began to display the same types of behaviors that he had right before going to rehab which was unnerving and frightening to me.

One night shortly after walking out on the job, we were at my dad's party and I realized Ben had been missing for an hour or two. We had both been drinking heavily, and I went outside to see if he was smoking, possibly, but I noticed that my car was gone. I couldn't get ahold of him on his cell phone because it was dead, and I began to panic. It was winter, and the roads were extremely icy and there was absolutely no reason for him to be behind the wheel of a car in the state he was in, but nothing ever seemed to stop him when he was in the moment. After another half hour of worrying, he casually strolled into the house like nothing was wrong. I was furious that he had taken off again because this scared me as it brought me back to the same fear and confusion I had experienced previously. He told me he had taken my car for a ride to do some donuts in the snow and had gotten stuck. Apparently, he was trying to do donuts in the middle of the road in the middle of the night and spun out of control and hit the ditch. He had tried to get it out, but the snow was too deep, so he walked the 30-minute walk back to my dad's without even a coat on. My vehicle was a BMW 320i and rear wheel drive. It was not the vehicle to be doing donuts in the middle of winter in let alone drunk donuts.

That next morning, my dad took us up to the spot where Ben had gotten my car stuck, and we managed to pull it out of the three-foot snow bank he had gotten it stuck in the night before. I was furious about the fact that he had driven the car while highly intoxicated and the fact that he had done serious damage to the car that there would be a hefty repair bill coming shortly. That week after bringing it into my dad's repair shop, we found out that he had broken the lower part of the radiator and got a quote to repair it. With my car being an import, the parts for these repairs were much more expensive than domestic manufacturers. The reason I had gotten a BMW was because I had received a large sum of money from insurance proceeds from an accident I had suffered when I was little. I had gotten the car before I even met Ben and could afford the parts back then. With the bleakness of our financial situation, we didn't have the money to do the repair, so we decided to sell it to my dad's dealership, and we would get by with using just one vehicle we had left, Ben's truck. It was sad for me as this was my beautiful car and I had taken care of it. It was just another incident that was adding to my resentment as the months went on.

Chapter 7

Throughout the rest of that winter, there were more occasions that Ben would go missing throughout the night. There began a pattern of arguments which led to him taking off in his truck, and he wouldn't come home until the next morning. He loved being in the mountains alone, so he would drive, usually drunk, up into the hills where he was surrounded solely by nature and bask in his loneliness and anger. We were both feeling tortured with each other and didn't know how to communicate effectively to make things better. We had tried counseling, but we both weren't fully committed to getting to the depth of our issues, so it was pointless.

When he would leave, I would feel lonely and isolated, so I would usually go up to my mom's house where I would stay for a few nights at a time sometimes. He would call when he got home from being in the woods overnight when he wouldn't find me at home the next day and then we would continue this blaming war with each other until one of us hung up and took some space before we decided on reconciling. It was another vicious cycle we couldn't manage to break. The funny thing about how I felt, though, was when we would get into these disastrous arguments after being at my moms for the night, I would always want to go running back to him even though I was so furious. I had this idea that we would run back into each other's arms after some of the worst fights, and we would embrace each other and fall madly back in love all over again, and it would be bliss. I was constantly searching for that fairytale feeling I had lost long ago. I would miss him terribly while we were apart, and I had to force myself to stay with my mom in order to make him see how his behavior had been affecting our marriage. At that point, I truly believed that the majority of our issues stemmed from his mental health and addictive behaviors.

After a few days, we would calm down and tell each other that we were ready to work on our relationship. I would come home, but there would still be resistance as we would brush the argument under the rug and try to go back to being OK with one another. We couldn't have possibly gone back to a normal, healthy relationship with all the resentment that had been building between us. I think we were just too afraid to address it for fear of the consequences.

Another major argument we'd been having was Ben's constant urge to hide his habit of pornography from me. I had never had an issue with this before, but since finding out about my dad's indiscretions, this had been a major sore spot for me. When I found out that Ben was casually watching pornography, I felt like this was another betrayal. When I asked him to refrain from watching explicit videos online, he supportively agreed that he would not do so anymore. I felt like he was beginning to understand where I was coming from and trying to be the partner I needed him to be. However, his commitment to his promise didn't last long because one day when he was out, I was searching through the history on the internet looking for a website I was trying to track down from a few days before and I came across a few porn sites that he must have searched for. I was disgusted and angry and verbally attacked him as soon as he walked through the door. He got his back up and defensively tried to explain that they were pop-up ads that came up without his control. I didn't believe him for a second. We were trying so hard to build our trust back, and it was another lie that would set us back even further. I felt like I couldn't trust him or count on him for anything.

For weeks after the pornography incident, there was even more toxicity in the house than usual. We were constantly at odds with each other and couldn't find a way to compromise our feelings in order to communicate through them. We needed some serious help but were too stubborn to accept it. We had come this far just the two of us, and I felt that we could work it out together if we both wanted it badly enough. I wanted it bad enough, but there was so much anger and animosity that it would have taken too much counseling to get through it. We didn't have the money or energy for the kind of therapy we needed. Thus began his accusations of my own addictive issues and behaviors. I was beginning to feel manipulated and began to consider my own drinking habits and how they affected our arguments. He would point out that he wasn't the only one with addiction issues and that I had a part to play in it also. I knew my past drinking habits were heavy through high school and my adolescent years before him, but I felt I was able to differentiate between how alcohol would affect his mental health and for me, I believed it was a social habit. My mom would always warn me growing up that I was predisposed genetically to alcoholism as it ran heavily in our family, but I always thought I'd managed to stay in control of it. *So,* I thought. I had never been under this amount of tension for a long period of time, and this stress was leading me to drink more heavily and frequently as I began to care less and less about the effects it had on our marriage. Ben too, was not shy about pointing this out. I started to feel out of control and drinking was a way of coping for me. I justified it with the fact that I wouldn't do the insane things that alcohol led him to do.

I was never really sure if Ben was experimenting with drugs again or if he stuck solely to alcohol. It wouldn't have surprised me if he was dabbling in them again because his behaviors were beginning to become erratic. He was still up and down with taking his medication, and our fights previously had never usually been so physical, mainly just verbally aggressive. There had been a few instances previously where they could have led to a more physical altercation, but back then we weren't in a damaged enough place where we would have put our hands on each other. It took until that winter to have our first physically abusive battle.

We had both been drinking through the evening, Ben was in one of his irritable moods, and we were under each other's skin since earlier in the afternoon. I wasn't surprised when he mentioned he was going to take off and get out of the house for a while. I was terrified of him getting into an accident or getting pulled over by the police each time he took off half-cut and was afraid of him losing his license again. It was imperative for him to have his license while he was still looking for a job. It had been a few months before he had quit, and the credit cards were starting to get racked to their limits. After threatening to leave, he went to the bathroom, and while he was out of sight, I quickly snatched his truck keys to hide them so he would be forced to keep from getting behind the wheel. I ran upstairs and hid them under my side of the mattress and lay on top of the bed like I was going to sleep. He came upstairs in a rage after searching relentlessly for them, accusing me of stealing his truck keys and ordering me to give them back. I spoke sensibly to him that I was tired and going to bed, and he must have misplaced them. I reminded him that he had drunk too many beers to drive anyway, and he shouldn't be out on the road in his condition. This infuriated him. He began to tear apart the room in search of his only escape out. He began searching through his clothes, looking through the blankets and under the pillows. He was slamming the doors of the bedside tables, exhausting all his options. Finally, he straddled me on the bed and held his grasp around my neck and threatened me to give them back. I had never seen him come to such an extreme reaction before, and it frightened me more than it ever had before. I repeated I didn't know where they were, and he lunged to the bottom of the bed and pulled me by my ankles toward him. I was enraged that there were no restrictions to his actions, and I began to fight back. I was beyond frantic and willing to do anything to defend myself at this point. I grabbed his hair and pulled him toward me while I kicked my feet into his chest. He grabbed me by my hair next and flung me toward the side of the bed, where my body hit the bedroom wall. He leapt up off the ground after he fell backward after throwing me, and he lifted the mattress up and pushed it over on top of me. He grabbed the keys and took off down the stairs and out the door before I could stop him. I climbed out behind the mattress disheveled and sat on the floor shaking and sobbing in disbelief of what had just happened. I looked around to find the entire room torn apart. I had let myself get to a level that I had never experienced in my life. I was angry and afraid and had gone into defense mode. I had not expected this aggression to come out of me towards another person, let alone toward my so-called soul mate.

I went to bed that night after putting the room back together and planned to go back to my moms in the morning. I knew this had reached a new level of destruction and that it wasn't safe any longer to be there.

That next day, I went to my mom's, where we had a few days of space from one another. It didn't take long before we ached for that longing feeling for each other, so I went back home. I don't think that my heart ached for what we were at the time, but for what I knew we could be. I was constantly yearning for that feeling again, but it was always clouded by the grievances. One evening, we had been arguing again after hours at the bottle, and I found myself once again pinned up against the wall in the kitchen with Ben gripping his right hand around my neck and threatening to cut me with a pizza cutter in his left. I don't recall what we were arguing about, but I do remember the fear of him being capable of doing many things I couldn't prevent, and I succumbed to his intimidation.

I had felt fear for so long that it was beginning to feel like my normal. I was living in a toxic marriage where neither of us could take control of the situation for the better. The petulance and abuse were far too deep to repair. I had been giving a lot of thought to looking into a divorce, and I had even threatened him with it a few times. I couldn't take the toxic environment at my job with the real estate team any longer, so I applied elsewhere and eventually started a new job at an accounting firm which was located right next to a lawyer's office. I knew one of the lawyers working there specialized in family law and mitigation. I also knew if Ben ever found out that I was going to see a lawyer, he would have tried to sabotage the meeting, so I knew I had to do it secretly. I booked a free consultation during one of my lunches and headed next door with a notepad and pen ready to take in as much information as I could.

I returned home after work the day that I saw the divorce lawyer and felt like I had some kind of ammunition if we started getting into it again. Sure enough, we were arguing, and I brought up my meeting with the lawyers. I brought out my notes to prove that I wasn't just saying I had gone, and I had some actual confirmation of my visit. I didn't go see the lawyer because I was trying to hurt Ben or blame him for our issues, I was tired and fed up with how we could never resolve anything, and the problems kept returning and getting worse. I knew we both had a part to play, and we were both to blame, but I didn't know how to cope with his outbursts, the physical aggression and his instability with his medications. These were all recipes for disaster. I didn't want to tell anyone about the physical abuse either, because I knew it would put more pressure on me to do something about it. This was my way of trying to figure it out. I was prepared to solve the issues on my own.

One night shortly after, there was a somber mood in the house because we both felt like we were defeated. We were trying to fix things on our own, and we should have enlisted more help. We were both too stubborn. There wasn't too much conversation after the lawyer talk, and I went to bed each night feeling like there wasn't much hope for our future. It was so common for me during those months to go to bed feeling helpless and with a sadness that wouldn't lift. Sometimes I would cry myself to sleep, trying to hide my face in the pillow so Ben wouldn't notice or hear me. I think he did often, but we were so broken that I don't think he could allow himself the vulnerability to reach out to me. It was a scary feeling to allow myself to be vulnerable during this time too. So many nights I wanted to reach out to him and for him to hold me, telling me we would be OK. My body wouldn't let me physically reach to him, my fear and resentment always held me back. I had a longing to be close to him; but we were so mentally and emotionally far apart. There was too much healing that had to be done first.

The morning after the divorce bombshell, we had breakfast together, and it was quieter than normal. I think the reality of having gone to see a divorce lawyer and taking that step had hit us both pretty hard. We decided that for us to really have the mental capacity and willingness to work out our problems, we knew we had to stop drinking again. It was a cycle that was becoming all too familiar once again, but I was relieved to hear that he offered this solution. I didn't hesitate, and I wanted to stop lying to my family. That morning, Ben confessed something to me that he had never told a single soul in his life. In order for us to move on whole heartedly, he wanted to be completely honest with me about something he had been holding onto for years. He told me that when he was living in Australia for six months, a few years before I had met him, he had been heavily using drugs and alcohol. One night, when he was high on cocaine and ecstasy, he had a sexual experience with another man. He would not tell me who it was, but it was someone he knew from back home that he had run into while in Australia. He said he wasn't gay or bisexual, but it was the drugs that made him want the experience.

I felt like a load had just been dumped on me, but I wanted to hide any kind of shock or surprise that I was feeling because I knew the shame he would feel if I did show it. I had questions and I asked with caution, to which he answered truthfully and openly. I was curious to know who the man was, but part of me didn't want to know in case I did know this person. I hugged him and felt in that moment that he needed support. I knew this information made him feel fragile and completely exposed with telling me because it was powerful information if I were to hold it against him. I knew he wanted me to keep it to myself, and so I did. It was another bomb that had been dropped on me once again, and I knew I had to be his strong support. He felt relieved that he had gotten it off his chest and was not hiding anything from me now, and we could now work through everything together. The part that bothered me was that I didn't feel like we were working through anything together. I couldn't express any concerns or insecurities this information brought me because I was still walking on eggshells around him and was hesitant to upset him.

This information not only led me to more questions but also questions regarding his faithfulness toward me. I knew I had formed some trust issues revolved around my dad's cheating history, and I hadn't fully addressed them yet. This was another point of concern in our marriage; trust. There was certainly a lack of trust on Ben's part when he would eye me from outside a bar and watch me to see how I acted with my friends, or when he would drop me off at work and wait outside to see if I would have a ride come pick me up to take me out partying for the night. All these situations started to add up for me, and I began to wonder if the reason he was so untrusting of me was that maybe he was the one who couldn't be trusted all along. I wondered casually from time to time if he had cheated, used drugs, or betrayed me in any other sort of way. Like my mom had questioned my dad over the years, I was now beginning to question my own husband. I was beginning to feel more and more insecure and inferior to the types of experiences Ben had lived through and the more I found out and tried to keep up with this erratic lifestyle, the more I realized I couldn't. There was no comparison between the kinds of experiences he had had and what I had growing up. My most extreme experiences were illegally sneaking into bars on the weekends before I was of age. I'd never dabbled in cocaine, had sex with a girl or done any extreme criminal activity. The only thing I could really compare myself to him was the depression and anxiety. This made it even harder to understand him and connect with him as we continued our marriage together. Ben's depression was something he suffered from even before I knew him. My depression didn't even compare to how bad his had gotten in the past. Before treatment, he told me he was depressed to the point of being suicidal. He had told me that one night, after being out drinking, he felt like he didn't want to go on living. He sporadically jumped into his truck, started out on the highway at excessive and dangerous speeds, and lifted his head out the sunroof window while holding his foot on the gas. His plan was to drive into a light post in which he would be decapitated. As he was driving erratically down the highway with his head perched out of the sunroof, his phone rang unexpectedly. It was his best friend, Mark calling. He said he just felt the urge to call. Ben answered it and slowed down as he brought his head back into the truck. He began sobbing as he explained what his intentions were for the night. That phone call had stopped him from ending his life.

Chapter 8

Our one-year anniversary was nearing quickly. May 25, 2009 was the day we would celebrate the highs and lows of our first year together. Everything we had gone through, we made it through together and it was something to celebrate even if we weren't drinking to toast the occasion. We made reservations at a five-star resort on the lake and sat out on the patio and took in the lake and mountain views. We had a lovely meal and discussed how we both felt accomplished with the fact that we had made it a year and recently were on the right track to turning our marriage around. This time we were prepared to stay sober and conquer any issues that lie ahead that we could tackle with a clear frame of mind. We had taken the house off the market for the time being until we could see some improvement in the real estate industry. It would have hurt us financially to sell and take a cut from the profits, which we hadn't estimated from the beginning. Dad was ok with this because we had planned on refinancing the mortgage to pull out the equity we'd gained to repay him in place of selling. We knew our mortgage payments would increase but now we had tenants in the front house to help out financially.

Ben had finally gotten a job and was working for a renovation company. He admired his boss and respected him, which was very refreshing. I felt more settled knowing he was enjoying his work and I was able to focus on my own work. We had just gotten a puppy and things felt like they were finally getting back to a good start. Even though we just had the one vehicle at this time, we were still managing to make ends meet and get by.

It was the beginning of June, we both had good jobs, and we had just adopted a puppy that completed our family of three. I had registered for a couple online courses through the college a month prior in order to begin my education in the business administration program. Things felt like we were moving on the right track and we were in a good place which meant Ben was feeling better. We were starting to see a little bit of light at the end of the tunnel and were feeling hopeful and optimistic. I was enjoying my new job at the accounting firm and felt like it was a career I could settle down into. For a few months now, it felt like we had turned a new leaf and we were getting somewhere positive.

With the toxicity and animosity wearing off slowly, it wasn't long before Ben started feeling better and began to consider trying to wean off his medication again. I was always weary when he tried to go off his medications, but I knew we were in a much better place this time, so I made a point of paying extra special attention to his moods and behaviors in order to monitor his progress. I could tell after a few days that his sleeping habits were starting to shift again. He would have more trouble falling asleep at night, which meant he would be extra tired in the morning and throughout the day. It was a cycle that I had become too familiar with time and time again, and it forced me to address it with him.

After about a week of weaning off his medications, I came home after work one Friday afternoon to find Ben sitting on the patio with a beer in hand. He always seemed to surprise me with a relapse and was acting like it was no big deal. He suggested that if I wasn't comfortable with the drinking, maybe I should stick with the nonalcoholic beverages because he had it all under control. I felt like I was starting to lose my mind again. I was beginning to think that I was the only one with the problem. As long as he had his drink, Ben didn't seem to mind the arguments and chaos that the alcohol brought into our home. There wasn't any way I could continue competing with this addiction, so once again I gave in. It was always a manipulation game to convince me that it would be normal each time, until it hit a new level of destruction. I knew there would be trouble ahead throughout the summer, but I was tired of fighting. I felt like the only way to possibly cope with the chaos was to indulge in the alcohol myself. The exhaustion had overwhelmed me, and I just wanted to feel relaxed the way Ben did with each new relapse. The very beginning emotions of a relapse always caused me tension and anxiety, which seemed to do the opposite for him. They say in AA that after each period of recovery can follow with a relapse that gets worse with each one and can eventually lead to death. This was my biggest fear, the fact that each relapse had gotten worse and that death wasn't that far of a reality.

That week predictably led to a series of arguments, outbursts, and nights alone in the house by myself. Immediately, Ben was back in the habit of taking off again and me not knowing where he was. I began to wonder if there was someone else he was taking off to go see because surely he and I weren't connecting and he couldn't possibly be sleeping all alone up in the hills in his truck.

One night during those next couple weeks, he stayed home, and we hadn't been fighting. I woke up to his phone ringing at three in the morning. Ben was fast asleep, and so I reached for his phone and found my sister's phone number on the caller display. I was stunned and confused as to why she would be calling him at three in the morning. I started looking through his text messages and found messages that read "I miss you" and what I would consider to be inappropriate messages between my husband and sister. I knew Maddy was still doing cocaine regularly, and I began to wonder if Ben was partaking in these threatening habits all over again. The anger and hurt came at full force as I read through each and every message that was exchanged between them. It wasn't clear that anything sexual had been going on, but at this point I wouldn't have put it past him. This was an ultimate betrayal by both of them, going behind my back and even having conversations that I was not aware of was hurtful. I couldn't sleep that night as explanations and situations circled around in my head but was too tired to start a fight in the early hours of the morning. There wasn't much time wasted in the morning before I demanded an explanation.

The hardest thing for Ben was admitting his faults. He knew he was in the wrong, but he couldn't admit it. I insisted on clarification from him, his back went up and he became extremely defensive. He justified himself by saying that he could talk to my sister in a way that he couldn't talk to me. She understood his addictions better than I could, and he could trust her for support. This didn't make any sense to me and gutted me as I came to realize he had been going to my own family before me. I didn't understand how an addict could trust another addict. I had a gut feeling that they must have been doing drugs together when Ben would run off after one of our arguments. It was such a feeling of deception to find out that they had a secret that I couldn't even relate to because I'd never done the drug myself. I'd never experimented with cocaine before and hadn't planned to, but I was beginning to feel like I would never fully relate to who he was as a person completely. I started to feel like maybe he was better off with someone like my sister, who struggled with the same substance abuse issues. My past experiences in life couldn't even compare to his. I was beginning to feel like I didn't measure up as his wife because I couldn't connect with what he'd been through as I hadn't been through any of it myself. We were the same but so different. When we were good, we were rock solid and no one could tear us apart, but when we were toxic, anyone could feel the vehemence energy between us from afar.

That week, the information I had found out about was a sore spot that I was still trying to process. The next weekend, we made a pact to stay on good terms with each other for the entire weekend. We still planned on drinking casually, even though we were in complete denial about our issues that came with the consumption. We still hadn't learned our lesson from the past episodes yet and both weren't ready to give it up completely.

There was a house party we were planning on going to with mainly all of my sister's friends, and we had been pre-drinking before we arrived. We'd only been there for an hour or so when I couldn't find Ben. I was calling and texting with no response. I couldn't have known where he went. Maddy was with me at the party, so I knew he wasn't with her. She pulled me into the bathroom, and I had to bring up the text messages. She told me the same thing Ben had told me, and it was a purely platonic friendship. She was just trying to support him as a friend. She pulled a bag of cocaine and a debit card out of her purse and arranged two lines of coke in front of me. She told me I could do a line and she wouldn't tell Ben. I hesitated at the thought of Ben finding out, but I felt like this was a way to get back at him. I took my first line of cocaine and immediately felt exhilarated. I felt on top of the world as I inhaled the drugs through my nose and left the bathroom feeling like I was no longer an outcast. When Ben returned, he began to explain he took a cab to go get more beer, and got dropped off at the beach after where he met a couple whom he got into a lengthy conversation with. He told me his intention was to go get more alcohol for the party, but he got sidetracked. None of this story made any sense to me. I knew he was lying, but I couldn't understand why, and who he went to see when my sister had been at the party with me. I accused him of going to see another woman, and he stormed off mid-argument. It was the same argument we'd been having, and I was tired of reliving it over and over again. Moments later, when I went to go find him, I found him at the side of the house with my sister in a corner explaining to her what had just happened. This fueled my anger even more. I accused them both of being inappropriate and needing to stay away from each other. This infuriated Ben even more, which led to him yelling back at me saying he married the wrong sister. He took off toward the road yelling that he'd had enough and left. I didn't even have the capacity to really articulate all that had just happened. So much for our pact.

Ben had left for who knows where and I was quickly distracted by the effect that the coke had on me, and it left me wanting more. I don't know if it was the series of events that went on that night or possibly the effects the alcohol and coke had on my brain, but I ended up making out heavily with one of my sister's girlfriends. I'd never had any kind of romantic relationship with another woman before, but it just happened that night. We found ourselves at the side of the house, in the bathroom, and in the backyard, making out. It was the wee hours of the morning before I got back home after my wild and adventurous night. I felt like I had just accomplished two experiences that I had struggled to identify with Ben over, and now I suddenly felt I had some sort of association to where his head was at and some relatability. Maybe this would allow him to finally equate with me, and we could work through it together on equal grounds.

That next week was the toughest week of our entire marriage. I hadn't considered the affect my actions would have on Ben entirely. I had naively hoped that by introducing myself to something he had struggled with previously, I would be more empathetic and compassionate with his addictions. However, this created even more fuel to the fire and caused an even bigger rift. I also had this idea that if he could dabble back in his cocaine habit, why couldn't I experience it too? We spent the next week arguing and trying to break each other down, insult after insult. It was the most toxic environment, and I hadn't even recognized the severity of it. When you are in a relationship that is so volatile and venomous, you sometimes don't even realize how bad it is when you're in the center of it. It was a marriage that had long been broken and would take a miracle to repair. There was no longer any intimacy, affection or words of encouragement. You could feel the toxic energy in our home, and everyone could see it. I just didn't know what it would take to break it. We were both in this painful and destructive environment we had created for ourselves, but we knew we both couldn't live like this for much longer and the need for a solution was urgent.

Chapter 9

It was the end of June, and my dad and a few staff members of his were planning a camping trip just a couple hours away at a campground called Mabel Lake. It sounded like a fun idea to get away from the house and hopefully try to have some distraction for a few days while trying to relax. I was even starting to feel the physical effects on my body with the constant battles. We had both always loved camping together, so we thought it would be a good opportunity to get out of town and enjoy the tranquility of the outdoors. I knew Ben loved camping, even though I knew camping was his way of allowing distraction and disconnection from the reality of our marriage. I had it in my mind that this was one last opportunity to try to reconnect in any way and to see if there was any life left in our marriage that we could repair. It wouldn't be long before we'd be forced to seek some professional advice to save our marriage. We had some much-needed decisions to make in the next steps of either repairing this marriage or going our separate ways. As despairing as our marriage was, I still couldn't imagine us separating and seeing each other with different people. It would have killed me. There was so much love that had been lost and I couldn't bear the thought of giving it up without trying everything I had to restore our union.

It was Sunday, June 28, 2009. Our last day at Mabel Lake, and we had packed up everything that morning so we could spend the day out on my dad's boat and take off that afternoon back home. We were all having a blast on the boat, drinking beer and blasting the music as we sped around the lake. It was a beautiful summer day, and we were sad to have to go back home. We'd had a really good weekend, with no fighting. None of us were concerned about how much we had been drinking that day, even though we all had to drive the two hours it took back home on the highway. I wasn't too concerned because I knew Ben was driving and I didn't have to watch what I was drinking. I didn't realize how much we all had consumed until we went to load the boat on the trailer. My dad had asked Ben to drive the truck with the boat trailer and back it up into the lake so he could load the boat on it. I didn't know if it was the beer or the inexperience, but Ben could not figure out how to maneuver the truck back with the trailer into the lake for loading. It took multiple tries before my dad had to hop out of the boat and do it himself. I was frustrated at this point because now I knew it was the beer that had impacted his judgment and I was giving him the gears because now he needed to drive home. We had agreed he would be the one driving, so he was supposed to be watching his alcohol consumption. I told him we would need to stay for the next couple hours before he could even consider driving, and that it was completely irresponsible of him to not even stop to think that he might not even be able to drive. I was now beginning to work myself up and take it all out on him in front of my dad and staff. Ben was getting defensive, and I could tell he felt embarrassed, so he immediately grabbed his truck keys and hopped in his truck as he yelled out the window to catch a ride home with my dad because he wasn't about to take me anywhere with him. I couldn't believe he was actually going to drive away with how much alcohol he had consumed throughout the day, but I assumed he was going to drive to another camp site or find somewhere not far away to be alone while he sobered up to drive back. I was fuming when I hopped into my dad's motor home with my dog, as I vented yet once again to my family.

It was nearing early evening as we made our way through Vernon, which left us with just about an hour until we made it home. I was still heated at the events that went down at the lake as we turned the final corner out of town and began our final stretch of the highway home. We could all see up ahead there was a lineup of vehicles stopped on the highway as my dad crawled to a stop. Nobody seemed to know what was going on, and it was strange that there was a pile of vehicles stopped for miles ahead of us. Once we stopped, my dad got out of the vehicle and began to ask people around us in their vehicles if they knew anything. Dad was walking back to the motor home when we saw a police officer making his way past each stopped vehicle, informing them of what was happening. My dad quickly hopped back into the motorhome and there was something that came over him that I could read all over his face. I panicked, as he told me that I needed to brace myself in case it was Ben that could have been in an accident. I didn't know where it was coming from when he said that to me, but he said he had a gut feeling, and he could feel it in his stomach that something was wrong. I told him there was no way it could be him because he had so many brushes with death and had too many angels around protecting him. I didn't want to let myself believe it could have been Ben, but my mind raced as I thought of the many possibilities. What if he needed to be in the hospital for months recovering after an accident like this...? Would he be able to work and earn an income? How convenient...what if he had months and months of recovery and was possibly paralyzed or had broken bones in multiple places? My head started spinning as I began to spin story after story in my head while my anger continued to rise at the thought of him driving after having drank so much. Not only would it be a long road to recovery but a long road to financial recovery, that we were finally just getting out of.

Once the police officer reached us, he informed us that there was in fact a car accident and he couldn't give us any details of the vehicle, but we were being rerouted, which meant we would have to turn around and go the long way home. As we turned the motor home around on the highway, following the multiple vehicles that had to take the same route, I considered all of my options if it were the case that it was he had been in the accident. My dad was concerned about the fact that there were vehicles for miles backed up and that they weren't allowing anyone to pass through, and that it must have been a pretty serious accident. We were turned around and headed home on the secondary parallel highway, when my dad received a phone call from one of his employees that had been ahead of us and had happened to pass by the accident site. He explained to my dad that he had seen it was a 1998 turquoise blue Ford F150, which is exactly what Ben was driving. Now I began to really panic. I still felt a little bit in denial because no one had confirmed anything yet, but my dad decided to call the police and explain our situation and informed them that he had suspicions that it could have been his son-in-law. They responded by telling him we needed to stop somewhere nearby, and a police officer would be by to speak with us. I could tell by my dad's reaction that it didn't sound good, but I hadn't even considered the worst possible outcome. I was dwelling on the fact that he was most likely hurt and had been possibly taken to the hospital with a few broken bones. Looking back on it now, I think if he was being rushed to the hospital, the police officers would have told us right then and there over the phone and wouldn't have made us wait for them to come and tell us in person. Little did I know, though, I had never been through anything like this before, so I hadn't really known what to expect.

My dad had a good friend from high school that lived about 15 minutes away from where we were, so he called him, and we pulled up to their place. They lived on a great big acreage and sold fruits and vegetables at their orchard. They came out as we pulled up, and we all sat together in the parking lot awaiting the police car that pulled up after what seemed like hours. I felt anxious to hear the situation so I could begin planning for Ben's recovery, but I was not ready for what he was about to tell me. I will always remember this police officer for as long as I live. He got out of his car, straight-faced, zero emotion, and headed straight for me. I got up to speak with him immediately as he made sure I was Krista, Ben's wife. I informed him that I was his wife, and he proceeded to tell me unsympathetically that Ben had in fact been in the accident and that he was pronounced dead on the scene. He had hit the meridian going much over the speed limit and had bounced off, throwing his truck against the rock wall that divided the highway from the hill, and he was thrown out of the driver's side window as he wasn't wearing a seatbelt. He had flown out of the window as the truck rolled a few times and had hit his head on the pavement, which caused internal bleeding and immediate death. The police officer explained that there were multiple beer cans spread across the highway from the box and interior of his truck, and that they would be performing an autopsy at the hospital to calculate his blood alcohol levels.

When he finished explaining the gruesome details, I couldn't speak. I was in complete shock and wasn't sure how to react. It didn't feel real, especially not the way the officer had just explained everything without any sort of emotion attached to it. I felt my dad's girlfriend come up behind me because she knew I would need the support physically and emotionally right then. I felt myself falling to my knees after I'd processed what I had just heard and, all of a sudden, felt like I had been hit in the stomach as the tears began to pour out of me. The officer didn't offer much empathy as he handed my dad a card where he could reach him, and following him was a grievance and support counselor, which they must have arranged for me immediately after. I knew I had to call Ben's parents, which would be devastating for the both of us, and I was terrified to make the call.

As soon as Ben's parents arrived at our location, they rushed out of their vehicle toward me as I fell into their arms as the guilt and devastation swept over me. I couldn't feel my legs as they buckled beneath me. I gripped on to my mother-in-law for support. I was awaiting the questions and was terrified of having to explain the situation to them and how it had all happened. It was all about to come full force at them, the reality of what had been going on for the past year and a half. I could feel their anger and confusion burning through me as I informed them of the fact that there had been alcohol abuse for a while. I couldn't even blame their anger as they were kept out of the loop, especially when they had done so much to support us and tried to support Ben's sobriety as much as they knew how. I knew Ben had felt like their involvement was too overbearing, but he wasn't doing everything he could to stay sober either. After the police and support contact from the survivor's ministry had left, my dad brought me back to my mom's for the night. I couldn't have been home alone and wanted to be with my family.

It was all such a blur of events over the next few days. My boss had given me the week off, which I needed, and there would be the funeral and legal matters to tend to. On the Wednesday after the accident, we had planned to drive out to the funeral home in Vernon to go view Ben's body one last time. The plans were to have his body cremated and the ashes would be scattered at the top of a mountain overlooking the city, which was his favorite place to be. I couldn't have prepared myself that morning to go into that room to see and feel his deceased body. I had been numb upon waking that day, preparing myself mentally for what was to come over the course of the next week. I planned to drive out with Ben's parents and my mom, who suggested I take some Ativan to calm my nerves for the viewing process. I couldn't speak or think as we drove the hour and a half to the funeral home. We were driving on the same highway that Ben was lying dead on just under 72 hours prior. I couldn't bring myself to look at the wreckage marks on the highway that imprinted his death just days before. I couldn't envision him lying on the road, being flung through the driver's side window and hitting his head so hard he had died on the spot. None of us spoke on the drive much as we waited with anticipation to view our reality that morning.

We arrived at the funeral home and were greeted by the director, who offered me the first viewing. I had been unsure if I wanted to view him because I hadn't viewed many dead bodies in my life and I was afraid of what I was going to see. I had given it some thought that morning, and I didn't decide until we arrived there. I wanted to see him in whatever shape or form he was in, because I didn't want my last memory of him to be from the day we had been arguing and the anger I felt when I looked at him would be the last. I needed some kind of physical closure.

They allowed me to go in alone, and hesitantly I made my way through the doors toward the table where he lay. I slowly walked up to his side and examined how he looked. For some reason, I didn't feel nervous when I saw him, and it was like all my fears had dissipated. He looked so peaceful lying there, completely still. I could see the bruises on the left side of his skull where his head had hit the pavement. He had bruises on his arms and most likely other places that I couldn't see that were covered by his clothes. His hair had been neatly combed, which was something he rarely did himself, and his face looked so vacant and distant. The emotions I was feeling came full force, and once again, I couldn't feel my legs as they buckled beneath me. I took his hand in mine and they were cold to the touch.

Everything about him was so lifeless. This was when the reality of the situation had hit me like a brick and everything in front of me seemed surreal. As I processed everything that had happened in the last few days, I laid my head on his silent chest and cried into him as I realized my life had taken me on a completely new road I hadn't paved out.

There was so much that I wanted to say to him and take back so many things I had thought and said over the last year and a half. He was gone and was never coming back.

At times, our marriage had gotten so bad that I had wished that he would leave, but I had never expected this to be my reality at only 23 years old.

The next few days were another series of blurred events. I don't recall much in between the day I viewed his body and the day of the funeral. On the day of the funeral, I had been hanging out with Ben's longtime best friend in the morning, reconnecting with him. It felt like I was connecting with a part of Ben. We drove together to the funeral, where I knew I would need the support, so I was glad to have him there. We arrived at the top of Knox Mountain, which is a well-known sightseeing and hiking attraction. It has beautiful views of the valley surrounding it, and it was the perfect location to honor his memory. It was a beautiful ceremony, and hundreds of people had been there to show their support and love. It was the place where I felt I was able to outwardly mourn the torment that had caused so much pain in our relationship, the battles we faced through addiction, and all the anger and contention that had ultimately led to the death of my husband and the death of our marriage. It was at the very end of the prayer that was concluding the ceremony when I noticed an eagle soaring above our heads in circles. I knew it had to be Ben watching over us because he had always been a bird lover. It was the sign I needed to see to know that he was in a much better place, and I knew he was at peace. He had battled depression and addiction for so long that it was almost a relief to see he was finally in a better place. There would be no more battles for sobriety on Ben's part, but I was blind to the fact that I would be fighting my own battles with drug and alcohol abuse for the next few years to come. This was where my worst fears for Ben became the reality in my own life.

Chapter 10

Over the next few months, my entire existence became a whirlwind of going to work, bringing a bottle of wine or vodka home, chugging it in order to become numb to the world, and repeating the cycle over and over. I went through so many emotions after Ben died. I felt a fierce amount of sadness, guilt, remorse, anger, and fear just to name a few. I could not manage my feelings and I didn't know where to begin trying. I couldn't shake this feeling of vulnerability and being left alone in the world, which soon became my biggest weakness. I was vulnerable in a way that I hadn't known I could be. I soon began relying on men that came to my rescue, whether they cared about me or not.

It began immediately right after he died. The night of the funeral, I found myself in such loneliness and vulnerable despair. I numbed myself entirely with vodka and found myself waking up in Ben's best friend's bed the next morning, realizing what I had done the night before. I didn't even really feel fazed about it. I had just slept with my husband's best friend on the night of his funeral. How could I have even brought myself into this situation when we were considered to be soul mates even throughout the vicious arguments and abuse. It was just the beginning of allowing myself to get swept up in the chaos and succumbing to the conclusion that alcohol and drugs would be the only thing that could numb me for survival.

That wasn't the only sexual encounter I exposed myself to right after Ben passed away. In the two weeks I had off after the accident, while I was supposed to be healing and grieving, I booked a flight to Calgary to go stay with one of my best guy friends. Prior to my marriage to Ben, I longed for a relationship with one of my best friends, whom I felt like was my first love. We could never find the right timing to form a relationship between the two of us, but he was someone I used to share everything with. He was the closest male friendship I'd ever had with anyone before my marriage, and I longed to feel that while I was in his presence again. When Ben died, I craved the intimacy of someone I could trust and hold on to while I struggled to pick up the pieces of my life. I spent three days with him, and when I left, I fell into an even lonelier despair than I felt before arriving.

I had begun a routine of drinking myself into oblivion every night and had no control over my actions, nor did I care. This is what began my spiral out of control as the night after the funeral haunted me for weeks but also in some way kept me connected to Ben that I could not let go of. It was sick, I know. I didn't understand the thoughts and feelings that I later believed to be the grief process that I suffered through. Not only did I suffer the anxieties and sorrows of my loss, but the financial struggles that immediately lay before me began to become a scary realization. I was now the sole owner and landlord of a rental property and had the financial burden of paying back my dad, which lay entirely on me. Even though we had mortgage insurance, which would pay 50% of the outstanding mortgage out, I was hesitant about receiving it due to the exclusion in the policy with Ben's blood alcohol levels at the time of death. This exclusion stated if the deceased has a blood alcohol level that surpassed the legal limit, that will deny us from receiving any money from our policy unless we had been paying the premiums for 24 months or longer. We had been paying our premiums for only 21 months at this point, and Ben's blood alcohol level was 0.34%, which was almost 4x the legal limit. Needless to say, after months of waiting anxiously for the results, I was not entitled to any proceeds of insurance money other than the Provincial vehicle insurance death benefits.

Having this financial burden all of a sudden solely on my shoulders was a pressure that I could not cope with on my own, along with just having lost my husband at such a young age. From my early childhood, I had taught myself to hide my emotions and stuff my feelings. Over the years, I became numb to a lot of my emotions and wouldn't allow my feelings to speak up. I hadn't learned how to deal with the hard issues in my life, so I learned how to self-medicate and numb my world around me. I began doing this with alcohol and drugs, and after Ben's death, I began to self-indulge like I had never done before. It didn't help that my best friend at the time, who was my tenant right on the property, was one of the major influencers that I would go to since before the accident. Her boyfriend had just broken up with her shortly after Ben had passed away, so we were drawn to each other as support systems, but it was a toxic support system between the two of us. We were both lost and looking for a path to guide us, but that path we took led to endless nights of partying, drugs, and incoherent sexual escapades. One night, she had a few friends over and they had brought an assortment of drugs with them. I was already hard into the alcohol and cocaine that night when I began snorting crushed ecstasy off the countertops. As I ingested more cocaine throughout the night, I found myself blacking in and out, although that was a normal occurrence for me, it seemed.

There were about five of us, and the effects of the drugs were hitting each of us hard. We all stripped down to our underwear and basically began somewhat of an orgy in her living room. The last thing that I remember is lying on the sofa caressing the privates of a little man while going in and out of consciousness. The next thing I knew, I was waking up the next day in my friends' bed with someone's hands down the front of my pants and not realizing where I was or who I was with. It was dark by the time I had woken, and I figured it must have still been early in the morning for it to be dark out. I was confused as to who was lying beside me and was thrusting their fingers in and out of me. At this point, I was still really groggy, but I knew I hadn't given anyone permission to put their hands down my pants. I pulled his hands out from under me and I recognized it was one of the guys who had been partying with us the night before. I didn't even remember him coming into the bed with me, nor would I have allowed it if I had been sober. I rolled over to grab my phone to check the time when I realized it was early evening and that I had slept through the entire day. I jumped out of bed and went through the back yard to get to my house to find my puppy had trailed toilet paper all throughout the house and he had been waiting all day for me without any food or water. I felt sick to my stomach and the ultimate shame and guilt I had ever felt. It was a Sunday evening, and I had made plans with a friend that week to go see a movie, and I had completely bailed. I knew I had to work the next morning and I had just wasted my entire day and let people down again. I couldn't bear to face the reality of my decisions I was making and the shame and remorse I felt after what I had put myself and my body through. There were multiple accounts of this kind of abuse I was doing to my body where I would wake up in the morning and not know who I had brought home or what I had done with that person. One morning I woke up in my bed and could barely walk. I could recall bits and pieces of the night before but couldn't make out exactly what had happened. Apparently, I had brought home one of my tenants' old friends, and we had anal sex but I hadn't remembered any part of it. I was so oblivious of the harm I was doing to my emotional and physical state that I found myself with this same guy and two others in a foursome the very next weekend.

I knew this wasn't a healthy way of dealing with losing my husband, but I wasn't ready to face my own fears and demons. My choice was to distract myself throughout the day and drown myself in alcohol at night and wasn't afraid of where that might lead me. It was a harmful routine that I had relied upon and didn't have the courage just yet to conquer it on my own. I knew I was not only harming myself but my family and friends that were rightfully concerned about me.

I began seeing a drug and alcohol counselor to try to gain some insight into my situation. Funnily enough, he was Ben's sponsor when he first came out of treatment, so he knew our history, which was a benefit for me. I went to our sessions for a few months, and I do believe I gained some insight from our discussions. He would challenge me to begin writing in my journal about how I was feeling a few times a week and to write when I had the urge to drink or do drugs. He wanted some insight into what was going through my head during that time. Another thing he confronted me with was challenging me to go a full week and a weekend sober. This was very difficult for me since this was one of the peak times of my anxiety. However, the alcohol and drugs completely worked against my struggle to cease my anxiety, but at this point I wasn't exactly willing to surrender either. I think in the entire time that I went to see him, I had achieved a week's worth of sobriety, and it felt good. I wasn't strong enough at this time to continue on the recovery train, but I had proven to myself that I knew I could do it if I wanted it bad enough.

This financial burden and the pressure it put on me at only 23 years of age was more than I could handle. I had so much support but chose not to lean on it. Ben's mom and dad were a constant in my life as much as my own family. They were going through their own grieving process, and I needed them as much as they needed me. I could feel their hurt and anger but the shame of feeling their pain was even more unbearable than my own… Rather than coping and going through the necessary grief process, I chose to continually paralyze my thoughts and emotions with anything I could find that would take away the pain even for a short amount of time. This also included my relationships over the next few months with men. I had met a variety of different men during this time, and I always seemed to attract men with money that I thought could financially take care of me in ways that I allowed in return for my affection and attention.

It was the fall after Ben's death, and I met this guy at a bar one weekend I frequented who instantly fell for me. He was about ten years older than me, and he showered his wealth in my direction immediately. I wasn't overly interested but he was pursuant and ended up coming back to my place with me. The next morning, he took me to a jewelry store where he let me choose a gemstone ring and the cost wasn't an issue. He took me shopping for clothes, out for meals, and spoiled me with many gifts. I wasn't used to this kind of treatment and the lack of concern for price tags. The only problem was that I didn't have any real feelings for him. I hadn't had any emotional feelings for anyone since Ben, but I also knew it was much too soon for me to have any sort of feelings for anyone. However, I couldn't seem to refuse any of the gifts he offered either.

We began casually dating and after a few weeks he whisked me away to Las Vegas for four days. I was looking forward to this trip and getting out of town, but I knew I would have no money for spending. The only asset I could quickly turn into cash was my engagement ring. I didn't give it much thought before I took it to a local jewelry store looking to sell it for cash. I hadn't considered selling my engagement ring until that point, but I was desperate for some quick cash for my trip in case of emergency. I brought it in, anticipating getting a few thousand dollars for it, because I knew it had cost over $6,000 when Ben purchased it. I walked out with $1100 cash for my trip to Vegas without blinking an eye.

I had been looking forward to getting away and a break from my reality. I was ready to go experience Las Vegas, where I could distract myself from the anxieties and pressures of my current situation. I never had any real feelings for this man but was eager to get away with him in order to get away from my world. It didn't take me long to realize how wrong this decision was.

We spent four days in Vegas, and it was one of the most amazing places I'd ever been. It was an adult playground with zero rules, it seemed. We walked the strip, went to some incredible shows, and ate delicious food. The only thing that was missing was my late husband. He would have loved it, but it would have been too tempting a place for him.

It was the day before we were leaving to come back home, and we spent the entire day at the pool. We were staying at Caesar's Palace, and they have a beautiful pool area where we swam, drank, and ate all day long. As the late afternoon approached, I noticed a black man attempting to get my attention but I couldn't really focus and was highly intoxicated from all the cocktails I'd had. Jay had gone to play roulette and I was alone, so this guy must have thought I was by myself. I wasn't paying much attention to where Jay was at the time, nor did I have the capacity to process what was going on, but before I knew it, this guy had his tongue in my mouth. I wasn't in a state of mind to comprehend what was really happening, and I felt myself blacking out and coming to as we carried on in the pool. Things were moving too quickly and getting carried away while Jay was gone gambling inside the casino. As I came in and out of my drunken consciousness, I was suddenly stunned that this man had inserted himself inside of me while we were in the pool. There was absolutely no way his actions were consented to because I couldn't have even spoken clearly without slurring my words at this point. I can remember, as I came to, pushing him away, but he would not back down. He held on around my arms and kept me in a position that I couldn't break free from. Both the effects of the alcohol and the heat had gotten to me, and I didn't have much control as Jay was nowhere to be seen. I was beginning to panic through periods of blacking out and felt like I needed to go back to the room to sleep it off and get some clarity because I knew it was a bad situation I was in. As I tried to break free of his grasp, he continued to thrust himself into me. Once I got the strength to push him off, I swam back to our towels and climbed onto the chairs. I was immediately embarrassed as I hazily sat out of the pool and realized that the other guests sitting around must have seen us.

As I sat curled up on the lounger, Jay casually strolled back to our spot and could tell something was wrong. I explained to him what had just happened and that I wanted to go back to the room. I needed him to bring me back there, but he had become angry at what I'd just done. He began accusing me of allowing this to happen and pointing out that I clearly wanted it as much as my assaulter. I couldn't understand how ruthless he was being after how I'd just been taken advantage of. I stormed off and had one of the security guards at the hotel walk me back to our room, where I slept off the alcohol for the next couple hours to sober up.

I woke up groggily around 7 pm to find Jay in our room. I was grateful to see him, until I realized that behind him was the same guy from the pool. I was confused and still a bit dazed, but Jay was clearly still very upset. He looked at me with a sneer and told me to have fun as he left out the door. He made a comment on his way out that I was clearly more interested in this other guy than him, so he had brought him to me. I was dumbfounded and afraid because we were in a closed-door room together and clearly he had more power over me and could take advantage of the situation. It wasn't long after Jay left that he had pinned me down on the bed and began to tear at my clothes and tell me that he wanted to continue what we started in the pool. He clearly hadn't understood that I wasn't interested even with the security guard accompanying me back to the room earlier. I told him I was exhausted and didn't want to continue anything, but he wasn't taking no for an answer as he continued to pin me down. I immediately went into fight or flight mode and had to tell myself that I needed to pretend to play along in order to get out of this situation fast. I went along with him and told him that if he wanted to have some fun, I would need to shower and get ready for the evening, so I would look my best and then we could have some fun. I don't know what possessed me to make this compromise so quickly with him, but I knew I hadn't intended on keeping this promise. He agreed as he backed off, and I hopped into the bathroom and locked the door behind me. I was unable to process what had just happened and my mind was spinning. I didn't know I was capable of coming up with a distraction while I was in panic mode, but it had been successful. I took my time in the bathroom and got ready as

I prepared myself to exit the bathroom door and immediately escape out through the adjacent hotel room door into the hallway. I had to gather enough courage to pull this off; otherwise, I wouldn't be able to have control over the situation as he was much stronger than I was.

Once I was finished, I grabbed my things that I needed from the dresser and said I had a few more things to do in the bathroom until I was ready to have some fun. I had to keep playing along. Once I had gotten myself together and brought up the courage, I opened the bathroom door and immediately opened the hotel room door and stood in the hallway where I ordered him to exit the room. I had one hand gripping the door casing and the other clutching the door handle, so if he did try to physically persuade me back in, I would have some sort of support. He was confused and urged me to come back in, as he pulled at my arm and began to become physically aggressive with me. I threatened him that I would yell and make a scene if he didn't leave the room, to which he did end up exiting and following me down the hotel corridor until we reached the elevator. I told him I didn't want any part of what he was expecting, and we went our separate ways as I headed toward the hotel lobby where I found Jay with his mom, who had come along with us on the trip. I was trying to hold back the tears when I reached them, but he began to express his sheer disgust at what he had thought I had just done and called me every name that made me feel the cheapest and lowest I had ever felt in my life. I was so embarrassed and hurt that he had orchestrated the entire thing, and the shame I felt was paralyzing. I wanted nothing more than to go home. I knew we were leaving the next day and figured if I could hold out until then, I could get home and never had to speak to this disgusting person ever again. The next day we boarded our flight and I had zero hesitation when I flew back home and left the airport vowing never to see him again.

This was not the first of many crazy and senseless experiences I would encounter over the next few years. I started to believe that because I was constantly living in a state of pure chaos which I believed was completely out of control in my life, that those types of relationships and situations kept coming my way.

After I ended things with Jay, my friend and tenant introduced me to one of her guy friends, who I instantly connected with on a friendship level. He was interested in me, but I couldn't find the feelings that I could reciprocate. We began seeing each other and the more interested in me he became, the more my walls went up because I enjoyed spending time with him as opposed to my last previous experience. It was a relief to not have the pressure or the drama. A little while in, he confessed to me that he had just been released from jail not too long ago for drug dealing. He was a cocaine dealer and ended up getting arrested in a trap the police had setup for him. I knew this wasn't the sort of person my family would accept after everything I'd been through, and it wasn't the type of environment I wanted to be a part of so I eventually broke it off before it got any further. It wasn't long before the next powerful influence in my life came along, though, and stole me away from him.

I was out at a local bar with some friends when I was introduced to this seven-foot-tall character with a handsome face and the biggest smile I'd ever seen. He certainly didn't waste any time before he pounced on me and asked questions about who I was, and why he had never met me before, and if he could see me again. I'd never been approached quite so intensely before and was flattered by his assertiveness. We had barely said hello to each other before he was planning our first date. I was extremely hesitant because this was only October, just 5 months after the passing of the love of my life and I continued to allow myself to be involved in these irrational relationships. I figured he probably had some kind of relationship issue because he was extremely pushy with me straight from the get-go. I reluctantly agreed to give him my number, and he contacted me that same night. He began contacting me every day for the next week, and I was feeling lonelier than ever, so I figured I would accept his invitation to a date. Worst case scenario was that it was a bust, but overall, it was a welcome distraction from my everyday life that I clearly couldn't maneuver through on my own. I had been so afraid to be alone during this time of my grieving process and was also terrified that my family and Ben's family would be judging me for jumping into these unimportant flings that never lasted. I was only 23 and I didn't understand what the grief process was supposed to look like or how I was supposed to behave. I felt ashamed that I had become so vulnerable that I had allowed these men to control me with their financial situations and power. I didn't have the confidence or self-worth to see past it.

I, again, had never had any real feelings for him, but once I agreed to see him, he showered me with gifts and financial support right off the hop. I didn't have a vehicle at the time, and he had lost his license so he allowed me to drive his SUV. This was a huge help for me financially, and he knew I needed the help. He knew I wasn't completely in it as much as he was, and I felt the pressure immensely from him as he would try to convince me daily that it was time for me to move on. When I hesitated if he'd make plans for us to go away or take me to extravagant events, he'd try to manipulate me by making me feel guilty because he was taking care of me financially to some degree and I should reciprocate. He looked at it like he was my knight in shining armor after a rough breakup that had come to sweep me off my feet. It wasn't long before I came to realize that he was always holding this power over my head, so I would feel obligated to him, which created even more anxiety for me. I wanted out so badly but didn't have the confidence or willpower to leave such a strong-willed person who made it impossible.

After a few months of dating, I knew I had to try to distance myself because he wasn't going to let go very easily. I began to feel like I did owe him my time and attention because of the gifts he had spoiled me with and his monetary support. I wanted so badly to part ways, but he was threatening and would bully me into staying. It was not a healthy relationship for me to even be in, and it contributed to my anxiety and depression even more.

During one of the last times that I had spent the night with him at his place, we had arrived back after being out with my mom and step dad at one of their friends' homes where they were hosting a party. We had drunk a lot that weekend, and it was a Sunday night, and I knew I had to work the next day, so I had cut the drinking to a minimum as the weekend ended. As we were laying down in bed, I heard this angry voice shouting from below us on the street, calling out his name. Over and over again, this person was intent on getting his attention, and kept repeating his name and yelled he was going to kill him. It terrified me because I didn't know who this person was and what he could have possibly done to him to cause this reaction. I wanted him to go to the window to check who it was, but he was intent on not addressing it. I wondered if it could have been another person with the same name in the building, but as I climbed out of bed to go check, he pulled me back and told me to stay lying down. It was almost like he knew who it was, and that terrified me even more.

Eventually, he stopped yelling, and I was fairly shaken up from the anxiety of it all. I went outside to the patio to check if anyone was still there but saw an empty street. It was an eerie feeling having someone call up to us, making threats, and I could feel the rush of anxiety pulsing through my body as I stared down the four stories to the street. It must have all been catching up with me at this time, and possibly the man yelling must have triggered something inside me, because I began to lose control of my breathing and I felt my entire surroundings closing in on me. My heart began to beat fast, and my hands felt clammy and began shaking. I had to sit down because I felt like I was going to pass out. I could feel my whole body go from one extreme temperature to the next within seconds. I was sweating, and then chilled to the bone, and everything around me started spinning. My ears were ringing, and I began to panic that I was either having a heart attack or I was dying. I hurried inside toward the bathroom, where I stripped off all my clothes and got into the shower, ran the hot water on me as I collapsed on the bottom of the tub. I didn't feel safe in

Michael's arms as he tried to console me, and I wanted to be alone. It was one of the scariest feelings that I had ever encountered, other than losing my husband months before. I knew I wanted to go home, but I knew I couldn't drive in the state I was in, so Michael drove me back to my dad's house, where I was living at the time. I had zero awareness of what my actions were doing to my mental state. I had never had anything like a panic attack before and hadn't recognized that the excessive drinking and heavy use of cocaine was having on my nervous system. It wasn't just the substance abuse that was compromising my mental health, but the recurring chaotic relationships I was managing to get myself into each time another one ended.

I had moved that fall to my dad's due to the fact that I wasn't able to financially support myself any longer on my own and I certainly couldn't cope with being in the same home where Ben and I shared our tumultuous marriage for so long. I called my mom on the drive home around midnight, and I explained the agony that I had just gone through. She calmly explained to me that it was most likely an anxiety attack and that I wasn't dying but still felt like I was. It comforted me to know that she too had experienced the same panic attack I had just suffered through and that I would be OK. We got back to my dad's house and went to bed. I knew the relationship I was in was causing me anxiety and it was just not a healthy place for me, and I needed out. I knew it wouldn't be easy to part from such a strong force, but I was determined to end it and move on. I knew Michael wasn't going to go down without a fight, but I was prepared to begin a healing process, and I needed to be on my own for that to happen. I felt like I was getting closer to knowing my limits and ending this pattern of false fantasy.

Chapter 11

Spring 2010, not even a full year after the love of my life had died, was when I realized the second love of my life was right in front of me...or so, I thought. Kyle, who was a friend of my tenant, was someone I had casually met when we were all partying together while Ben was still alive. Sometime during the spring of 2010, Kyle had reached out to me one night while I was cooking dinner. I thought it was a platonic text but hadn't realized he had other intentions for me. I had no idea that he had been interested in me from the beginning of us meeting, but it never would have crossed my mind either. We weren't communicating long before we made plans for the next time he was home to get together. Quickly, our friendship developed into a relationship that I never saw coming. I soon discovered I hadn't felt these feelings for anyone since Ben, and the urge to be with Kyle felt as strong as it had with my late husband. The problem, though, was that Kyle had been addicted to cocaine for many years already and it was not the type of relationship I needed at the time. The draw I had to Kyle was undeniably strong, as I adored him at the very beginning. His mind was so creative and open, and we had so many conversations I'd never had with anyone else before. We connected on such a deep level. It wasn't long before I began to realize that the relationship we had was largely surrounded by alcohol and cocaine, as I began to use more frequently with him at my side.

Those next twelve months spent with Kyle were a whirlwind of chaos and passion mixed with sadness and guilt that was masked by cocaine and alcohol abuse to a new level. I wasn't drinking and using cocaine to numb myself from my reality as much as I was constantly trying to calm the anxiety that I was suffering every day. Since Kyle had been using it for years already, he had more exposure and experience with it, so it never seemed to bother him to the extent it began to for me. It became more of a routine than just experimenting very quickly. Kyle worked out of town and would be gone for weeks at a time, and that left me to fend for myself since he was providing me with the drugs while we were together. It wasn't long before I found my own dealer that I was calling now on a regular basis. Stress and anxiety began to cloud my days as I tried to manage to make it through to the evening, where I knew I could bury it with a bottle of wine for a few hours. When that wasn't satisfying me, I began to make house calls throughout the week to my dealer, which turned into many sleepless nights. This was causing me even more anxiety because I would be awake until the early hours of the morning knowing that I couldn't go to work in the state that I was in.

The next twelve months were some of the craziest, most dangerous times of my life. Not only was I living on the edge, consuming unreasonable amounts of liquor and cocaine, but the situations and scenarios that I was getting myself into were taking me down a very destructive path. One night, a friend of mine that I had known for years had come into town, and we were out drinking at a bar as usual.

We went to this local bar that had live music and was known for a 50-plus age group. I loved going there because I loved drinking and partying with an older crowd. I never felt judged or looked down on like I had with some of my other peers. This night, I had consumed so far over the legal limit that I wasn't making clear choices. Kyle was with me, and we had been in the bar for most of the evening when it was nearing the end of the night and I could barely walk straight. I had to go to the bathroom, and I pulled Kyle in with me, dragging him into the stall and began to unzip the front of his pants. I knew what I wanted and wasn't willing to wait until we got back home. I recall someone being in the other stall right next to us, but I wasn't in the mindset of caring. They must have known what we were up to, as this was one of the tiniest bathrooms I had ever been in, consisting of two small stalls and a sink. Once we heard someone else come in, Kyle got nervous and pulled up his pants and quickly dragged me out of the bathroom and out of the bar before we could get kicked out. I left my friend in the dust. We headed toward the condo that we had just moved into downtown with my dad and decided to make a pit stop. There was a public fenced garden area with ponds, bridges, and koi fish swimming around, and we were feeling adventurous so we hopped the locked 12-foot fence to have sex in the gardens. We were making our rounds in the most public spaces and couldn't have a care in the world.

Many drunken nights out I can barely remember. One evening in particular, I had been partying downtown at an Irish pub I sometimes frequented, and I wound up in the early hours of the morning passed out in my vehicle in the back seat while the keys were still in the ignition. Some of the staff from the pub woke me up by knocking on my truck window. I had driven that evening, prepared to leave my truck parked and retrieve it in the morning, but I hadn't quite made it home. I was planning on driving myself home but hadn't quite made it further than putting the keys into the ignition.

One night in particular that I can remember, gave me a pretty eye-opening scare. Kyle and I were partying with some friends at the condo we were living in when someone brought out a bag of purified cocaine, and it was scattered on the kitchen island for open consumption. I had zero self-control and began to hit line after line in a short amount of time. After a few hours, I went into the bathroom to find someone sleeping in the tub, as I climbed into the shower. My heart was racing as fast as it could go, and I was beginning to hyperventilate. Kyle was trying to console me, but I felt sure I should have gone into the hospital because I'd consumed too much cocaine that I thought my body could handle. I was panicking and needed to cool myself off as I stripped down and hopped in the shower as someone lay there passed out next to me in the tub. I couldn't breathe properly and had to focus on deep breaths in and out. Eventually, I had calmed myself down and gotten myself into bed. By this time, it was already around nine in the morning and I had passed out until late afternoon when I woke up. I decided right then and there that it was the last time I would do cocaine. I had too many scares in the last few months and my anxiety was out of control, and that was a big enough scare to turn me from it for a while.

Living downtown was something that unquestionably contributed to my surge in alcohol and drug consumption as it was too easy to walk to the pub or bars that I frequently visited. The excessive amount of money I had been spending on alcohol was creating a quick decline in funds on a weekly basis. I found myself not being able to keep groceries at home, and I was constantly scraping together money for meals and fuel to get to and from work. I was prioritizing my habits before my needs.

I was slacking at work at this point and could barely keep it together. I would drag myself out of bed in the morning and barely get to work on time, trying to keep myself busy until lunch. At work, we had a room with a TV and a reclining chair that I would crash on during my lunch break. I couldn't make it through my day without taking an unprofessional afternoon nap. I could usually get away with this when no one was in the office. Sometimes my boss wouldn't come in for days at a time, and I would be the only staff member in the entire office. We shared space with another accounting firm, but they were slowly making their transition to a new building, so only half the time we were sharing our office space. This was another factor that contributed to my constant anxiety. We were located on the 9th floor of the building in a 2000 square foot office space with empty individual offices all around. I was mostly alone in the condo in the evenings since Kyle was away working and then I would come to work and be expected to hold down the office on my own for most of the week. My boss seemed to be struggling with his own depression and mental health issues, so he was finding if difficult himself to get to the office most days. I had to answer and take care of many phone calls and emails from angry and confused clients.

There was one day when I had an unexpected panic attack while I was alone in the office. It was extremely windy that afternoon, and I kept envisioning the building blowing over in the wind. Being terrified of heights, this made my anxiety worse, and I had to physically leave the building and get to the main floor to gather myself. My anxiety was causing me to have such unrealistic fears. I began to be afraid of so many improbable things that wouldn't necessarily have an effect on someone with a healthy state of mind. It wasn't good for me to be alone all day long and dealing with angry clients on my boss's behalf. I knew it wasn't the right work environment for me at this time, and I began my search for another company. I was hired as a bookkeeper, and there were many other firms in Kelowna where I could apply.

I eventually began my search, and within a few weeks I had gotten an offer. I hoped that by working in a group environment, I would be able to get a handle on my anxiety in a work setting and wouldn't have to dread going into the office each day. Even though I had cut back on doing the cocaine, I was still drinking almost every night to ease my angst. I can remember feeling so lonely in the condo by myself after a day at the office and needing someone there as support. I felt like a lost child who had no one but herself to rely on. I would sit near the window and look out on all the lights that lit up my downtown surroundings and cry for any sort of normalcy that I hadn't had for so long. I knew I hadn't grieved the normal way people do when they lose someone close to them, but I couldn't allow myself to go to that place, I wasn't ready. I was afraid to face my reality and choices I was making and wanted to stay in the victim mentality where it was my safe place.

It hadn't been more than a few months working at the new accounting office when I'd had the idea that I needed a fresh new start. My anxiety had calmed down a little but I still felt lost and wanted to change direction, which meant changing direction in a new province for me. My dad was dating a woman whose mother lived in Calgary and had offered me a room to stay in if I ever chose to move there. I was barely getting by financially and needed a break from the party scene. I knew I needed to leave the relationship with Kyle because he wasn't prepared to stop the partying, and I knew it was something I needed for myself if I was ever going to get a hold on my anxiety and life. I also had a couple of friends living in Calgary who I knew would show me around the city and get me familiarized. At this point, I figured I had nothing more to lose, so I wasn't opposed to taking such big leaps of faith to change the direction my life had been heading. I think the new accounting office I had started at a few months previous was giving me a new perspective on life without even having realized it at the time. I was surrounded by others in the office and had been happier with my new boss. It was a little bit of hope for a new routine and stability that I was looking for. I had a feeling though that if I truly wanted some kind of stability and fresh start, it would have to be in a new city and different environment.

It was coming up to the end of winter in 2011 when me, my dad, and his girlfriend planned to head to the big city for the weekend so I could see what it might be like to live there. The three of us piled into the vehicle one Thursday afternoon and headed onto the highway for the eight-hour drive ahead. I was excited to consider this as a brand-new adventure and chapter in my life after how many memories I had to live with in Kelowna over the past couple years.

It wasn't halfway through our journey when we pulled into a liquor store to get some beer and wine to make the trip a little bit more fun. My dad was driving, so I knew I had full range to drink as I pleased, and plus, I was on holiday after all. We arrived around midnight and pulled into Sylvia's mother's condo building and I could feel the excitement of the weekend ahead. There were so many more opportunities for me that I couldn't have back home. So many new people to meet and things to do. That weekend I partied with friends, toured the city, and it solidified my decision that this would be the change that I had been needing for so long. We got back to Kelowna that Sunday, and on Monday I explained to my bosses that I would be moving and had given them my two-month resignation. I wasn't ready to leave right away, but I planned it for the beginning of that summer. It was a bittersweet feeling because I had become close with my boss and his wife. I had babysat for them as I had loved spending time with their daughter, who was just a toddler. I would miss the friends I had made over the few months I had worked there with, but I knew I was just turning my wheels and going nowhere in Kelowna. My plan was to apply for the Business Administration Diploma at the University in Calgary and transfer the credits I had earned during my first few months into my first year at Okanagan College where I had attended online just before Ben had passed away. I would also work part-time as a server at a pub or restaurant, even though I had never had any experience serving before. This was an opportunity for a fresh start, and I was prepared to do what it took to turn my story around and create a new path. I could feel the new energy and excitement that lay ahead of me, and I knew what I had to do. I broke it off with Kyle without hesitation ignoring those initial feelings of lust and happiness I'd had with him just months before. I said goodbye to my family and friends without knowing when I would be back, and was prepared to make a new life for myself.

It was June 2011 when I packed up every belonging I owned and crammed them into my Jeep Grand Cherokee and headed out to a province I had barely visited and a city I knew nothing about. I said goodbye to my family and Ben's parents whom I had still been in touch with fairly often and hit the road. I had a bed to sleep in, but no job lined up and just a few hundred dollars to my name.

Within a week of moving to Calgary, a girlfriend of mine had gotten me an interview at a pub she worked at. Even though the interview was lined up, I knew I had zero experience in the restaurant industry before, but I was prepared to fake my way through because I knew I could pull it off. I knew nothing about serving customers and the systems that a restaurant would have in place, but I was determined to start making some money at any cost. I was hired and immediately started the following night, where I would have a few training sessions before I would be out on my own. It was a Friday night that I would be officially on my own tending the bar, and it was one of the busiest nights of the year. It was the NHL final game playoffs, and the entire pub was filled. I knew it would be a crazy night and didn't feel the least bit confident that I could handle an entire bar stand to myself, but I threw myself into it, and the night passed by in a haze. I was running off my feet until nearly midnight, but I had nailed it. I felt so confident that I had taken on this entirely new territory for me, and I was even good at it. I felt so relieved and knew that if I could handle one of the busiest nights of the year at the pub, I could handle any other shift they threw at me. I finished my nightly tasks, clocked out and sat at the bar with my new friends, celebrating a night accomplished and a bright new road ahead.

The fourth week into living in my new city, I knew I wanted to focus on enrolling myself in a college or university where I could transfer my credits and finish my diploma. I didn't have the appropriate credits to enroll at the university that I had planned on attending, so I did some investigating into transferring my credits over to one of the other local colleges that would accept them. I had to take an entrance exam in order to qualify to enroll in the Business Administration program which I had signed up for. I was prepared to start my program in the fall of 2011 and continue working part time at the pub. I prepared for the entrance exam as much as I could, but I had been out of high school for already seven years and my math and English studies were not exactly up to par as they once were, so I walked into the exam a little blindly. I took the multiple-choice exam but couldn't answer most of the questions correctly. It was a struggle to get through majority of the questions, in which I gave up halfway through and took guesses on the rest. It wasn't a surprise when I received the letter from the college that I had unfortunately not passed the exam but could sign up for a second attempt. I wasn't a hundred percent certain that this was the college that was right for me anyway. The disappointment from being rejected from the college made me even more confused and frustrated. My plan wasn't working out the way I wanted it to and wondered what I would do in a city where I couldn't necessarily start school immediately. I had a job, but it wasn't what I had intended for long term. I knew in order to pass the entrance exam I would have to study and possibly hire a tutor, and it felt like a lot of work. It was beginning to feel like I might have made a mistake. I had a good job before leaving Kelowna and was currently already enrolled in the business admin program, and I was already on the right path. It took me moving away to realize that. I had felt lost for so long and was hoping that by moving to Calgary it would open so many more doors for me, but it hadn't been the case. Working at the pub was a breath of fresh air but wasn't taking me down the road I wanted to end up. I wasn't prepared to stay and not further my career since that was the original plan for moving there. I was still searching for my place in life, and I hadn't found it in Calgary.

My experience in Calgary was short-lived, but I learned where I wanted to be. I knew I wanted to be back in Kelowna ready to begin the fall semester in order to complete my schooling. I had spent the last two and a half years since Ben had passed away lost and misdirected, and I felt like it was time I got my life in gear. I don't know what it was about moving to Calgary that gave me a boost to get my life sorted, but I knew I was wasting time at a job I wasn't passionate about and in a city that wasn't fulfilling me. I loved the big city and the opportunities that came along with it, but I still felt lonely and detached from what I knew I should be doing, and it took me some time there to realize that.

In mid-August, I gave my notice to my manager at the pub and began packing up my belongings once again. They didn't need a full two weeks' notice as I was only on the schedule for the next week, so on the day of my last shift, I headed into work with my Jeep loaded up as I did two months before, breezed through my last shift and hit the road. I was sad to be leaving the friends that I had made during my time there but was even more ready to commit to finishing my schooling and making a new life for myself where my family was. My time spent in Calgary made me realize that it was an experience I needed to have in order to realize that I was independent and could stand on my own two feet again. The experience that I took away from the restaurant was my motivation to work as a server back home so I could do my classes during the day. I was determined to go to school full time and serve in the evenings part time. This time I had it all worked out. I would just need to figure out where I was going to live and work when I got back.

My mom had been living in an apartment on her own that she had moved into a few months prior after she left my stepdad. They had had a rocky relationship right from the start, and she had decided she needed some time on her own to become independent and not to rely on another man. She had married my dad at the age of eighteen and had been married to him for twenty-five years. It seemed like almost immediately she had gotten into the relationship with my stepdad and hadn't necessarily spent enough time grieving and recovering from her marriage. Like my dad, my stepdad is also a recovering alcoholic. My mom had left one marriage that had been affected by alcoholism for another being affected by the same dependency. She spent the first few years of her second marriage wavering back and forth between leaving and staying. During one of her leaves of absence, she had gotten her own apartment, where she welcomed me to stay with her when I returned home from Calgary. I planned to stay with her for a few months until I could figure out accommodations that were more permanent. So, when I returned home, I unloaded my things and took up a room in her second bedroom. I immediately got organized and applied for my second semester of my first year Business Admin Diploma and applied for student financing. My next step was to search for a job, which I applied for at a steakhouse called Chop. It didn't take me long to find out that I got the job and I got into all my classes that were starting within the next two weeks. I felt like this was the right thing to do, and the pieces of the puzzle were finally starting to fall into place.

Chapter 12

With the amount of motivation I had with being back in school, I was starting to feel better about life and where I was headed. I had been doing well in my first semester back and had built confidence that resulted from the grades I had been achieving. I decided that being back in Kelowna, I would have to disassociate with any friends that I had done drugs with and try to focus on my studies and work. I had stopped using drugs; however, I was still drinking with friends on my weekends when I wasn't working. It was a hard decision not to go back to my old ways with the drugs but I knew it was a decision I had to make if I wanted to get anywhere in my life. I was beginning to feel different and more empowered when I would receive a good grade or did well on an exam. It was an accomplishment that I hadn't felt in years, and it gave me incentive to try to be better each week. I was putting everything into my schoolwork, and my grades had been reflective of my efforts. It was just after midterms when my mom informed me that she would be moving out of the apartment, back to my stepdad's and ending her lease. This is where I felt panic that I hadn't felt in a long time because I felt safe and secure living with my mom. The thought of having to find a new place to live on my own was a scary feeling because I felt like I was just starting to figure things out. I had a month to find my own place, but luckily my younger sister needed to find a place too, so we decided it would be best to live together. Right across from the college we were both attending, was a condo building where my uncle owned a unit that he had been trying to sell. It had been vacant for a couple years and it was still a bad market to sell in, so we made an agreement that my sister and I would rent it from him for a trial basis of six months to see how it went. He lives in Bangkok, Thailand, and he figured it might be a good idea to have some cash flow rather than having it sit empty and not sell.

On November 1st, we had moved into our new apartment, and we found a roommate to live with us. It was only a two bedroom, so my sister and I agreed to share a room to save extra on the cost of rent. She was so rarely there because she spent so many nights with her boyfriend, so it was beneficial for us this way. This savings allowed me to spend more time working on my studies without having to work extra to pay my bills. I was working at Chop only a few evenings a week and living off that income and my student loans. The restaurant was quite a different atmosphere than the pub I had worked at in Calgary. It was a higher-end steakhouse with higher-end clientele. This was a bit more intimidating for me because it put me out of my comfort zone. Being barely experienced as a server at a pub for only a couple months, it didn't give me the training and attention to detail that a server might have needed at this type of establishment. Not to mention my highly critical manager that added so much pressure on top of this made me insecure in my abilities to do the job properly. It wasn't long before I began to dread going to work. I knew I needed to make money in order to continue with my studies, but I began to develop such anxiety when I headed to work for a shift. The more I began to doubt my abilities, the more my manager would criticize my work and make me feel like I wasn't good enough to be working there. I knew it wasn't only me that felt this way, but I noticed she was picking every server apart individually. This was creating a very toxic work environment, and I had been so subjected to toxic environments in my life that it was not somewhere I wanted to be. I felt like I had no choice though. It was beginning to create a lot of anxiety again for me, and I had noticed that it began to affect my grades. I began to drink more throughout the week with my roommate, who I had become good friends with, and I began to drop more shifts and limit my availability until I was only getting one shift per week. This became stressful since I wasn't bringing in any money, but I also wasn't willing to take up any more shifts and work in a harmful environment. By Christmas, I was feeling like I was at a crossroads where I would have to make a decision. I knew I had to either continue to work my shifts until I could graduate or try to get another job and start all over again. Another hurdle I had thought I had tackled had become a new reality. I really struggled at this point because I knew what I needed but couldn't seem to get there physically or mentally. I had tried so hard already to remove myself from toxic environments and I kept finding myself back in them. I was searching for something in my life that could provide some sort of tranquility and grounding, but I just hadn't found it yet.

It was Christmas morning and my three sisters and I were spending the morning at my mom and stepdad's home opening and exchanging gifts. My oldest sister had flown in from Vancouver, where she was living and we had planned to be together as a family, which didn't always happen as we were getting older and beginning to have our own separate lives. My oldest sister had always been the spiritual one out of us, but I had never really shown much interest in her beliefs. Growing up Christian, I had never really searched for my own belief system and was told to follow what the Bible said but I never practiced much of it. It was a belief system that I had grown up with but always felt like I was disconnected with most of it and couldn't connect the dots quite like other believers I saw could. I had questions and wanted answers that nobody could provide that made sense to me. Maybe that is why I had never dug deeper into my spirituality, because I never felt drawn to it, but on that Christmas morning, I noticed my sister had gotten a book as a gift called "The Law of Attraction" by Jerry and Esther Hicks. Something about this book had sparked my interest. Maybe it was the cover of the book or the title, but I had been immediately guided to it. Maybe it was my own spiritual connection that had been lacking in my life that had reached out to me and made me pick up the book. I had never heard of this type of book before and how the Law of Attraction works, which is based on a positive mindset. At its core, the law of attraction is the belief that your thoughts create your experiences. The genres that I most enjoyed reading were autobiographies and memoirs which I did read a lot of, and I had been searching for something new to indulge myself in. I loved submersing myself into the dramatic lives of others and having a break from my own reality, which books had always provided me with. I had always been looking for any sort of temporary relief from my own environment that I had struggled with for the past few years.

For the duration of the Christmas break, I immersed myself in the teachings of the Law of Attraction to educate myself on this higher power belief system. It struck a chord with me, and I felt myself wanting to learn more and more. My life had not been going the way I had intended it to go for so long and I slowly began to understand the concept of changing my thought process from a negative perspective to a positive. The only person that was capable of making changes now was me. If I wanted to be able to quit my job, I would need to focus not on how miserable I was or wanting out, but to focus my thoughts to where I wanted to be. This book was also teaching me how to meditate for the things that would make me happy and bring me joy and peace. The Law of Attraction soon became the guidance that I had been looking for in order to have the confidence to make some real changes in my life. It wasn't an immediate response, but it took practice to put these methods into place. After my sister left back to Vancouver, I immediately went out to buy this book for myself to continue practicing and reading. It was like a brand-new way of life that I had been slowly transforming to and the book was exactly what I needed at the very right time.

In January, I started back at school with a new outlook. I tried to enforce this outlook when I headed into the restaurant for a shift, but I was still feeling so much anxiety around it. As I began making my way through the chapters, I learned about the power of meditation and visualizing my wants and needs. Through repetitive positive thought patterns and meditations that involve emotional connection,

I was beginning to see and feel a difference in myself. A few times a week, I would sit in the apartment in front of the largest window with the most sunlight and close my eyes to feel the energy working within. I would meditate on my intentions for at least 15 minutes at a time and focus only on the lifestyle that I intended for myself. I would visualize living in a home with someone that I loved and feeling free and excited about life. I would visualize coming home with a bag of groceries in the late afternoon, excited to prepare a meal for someone I loved. Cooking had always been a passion of mine and I had always dreamed of cooking extravagant meals for a family of mine one day. I knew exactly where I wanted this home to be. I also visualized a dog at my feet, specifically a Rottweiler which breed I had always loved, and serving myself a glass of red wine as I prepared dinner. The feelings I associated with this meditation were calm, serene, and peaceful. I longed to feel this way for so long, and I knew I had to create this reality for myself if I wanted it. Instead of focusing on what I didn't want, like working at the restaurant, I began to focus my thoughts again on what I did want. I wanted the freedom to work on my studies with a stress-free form of income. I started meditating on money coming to me with the feelings of joy and gratefulness surrounding it. I put this into practice for a month straight and began to feel hopeful. In February, I had a bit of a stumble. The winter months are always a bit depressing for me, especially this winter because it was extra cold and gray. I was walking home from my last class on a Friday afternoon when I could hear running footsteps behind me. A guy from my Business Law class had caught up to me and we began chatting. He was an attractive guy, a few years younger than me, but had these amazing piercing blue eyes, and there was something about him that had intrigued me. We walked the entire way to my apartment, and he asked if we could study together. I told him we could because that was what I intended to do that weekend anyway. I had no shifts scheduled as we had midterms nearing, so my weekend was open. It was like we had known each other because the conversation flowed so easily. I invited him to come up to the apartment and we could start studying right away, which is what my plan was anyways, but what I didn't plan on was him coming up to distract me with his good looks and charm. It wasn't even an hour before we both agreed to go back to his place and sip on some wine and have a hot tub. He had been renting a condo at a hotel timeshare across the lake in a more rural location. I went to this hotel as a little girl with my family, where we would go for Sunday afternoon brunches. It was a very desirable hotel back in those days, but over the years it had not been taken care of and was looking run down. As we pulled up to his place, it all looked so familiar. I hadn't been there in over 15 years. As we descended down the steep driveway into the units at the bottom of the hill, a flood of memories came over me. It was such an odd feeling to be here with him after so many years, with someone I barely even knew. We had just met, and he was taking me into his home where I would find out a little bit more about him. He captivated me, which is why I had agreed to come back to his place with him. I felt immediately comfortable with him, maybe because in a lot of ways, in the short amount of time we had spent together, he reminded me a great deal of Ben. Not the healthy and sober Ben, but the tormented, confused and lonely Ben. My heart went out to him, which must have been why I felt a connection. In the past, I had always been drawn to men with issues. I wanted to save them and cure them, but it was never a good idea for me. It must be why all my previous relationships never worked out, because I was searching for someone to save, but it was me that needed saving. It wasn't until later that I would understand that no one could save me but myself.

That night went by in a blur by as we consumed copious amounts of wine, talking about our pasts and having sex. I didn't plan any of it, but it just all flowed so easily and naturally. I got caught up in the moment of being in his presence, which so reminded me of my late husband that the desire almost became a need. I was longing for that familiar feeling that I'd lost so long ago, and it felt good just to live in it for a brief moment. The next morning, I woke up feeling like I had gotten right back to where I was a few years before. Emotionally caretaking a lost soul and taking care of his emotional needs before my own. He seemed so lonely and lost that I felt an urge to be there for him.

I spent the next few weeks with him, coming to his place and him to mine. I slowly began to notice he would go off the grid for hours at a time and I wouldn't hear from him for days. It was the same behavior that I saw with Ben right before he had gone to treatment. I started to realize that he had a drug addiction and it made me start to question if I should really be surrounding myself in this kind of situation again. It didn't take me long before I told him that I wasn't going to subject myself to this kind of behavior as I had suffered through these relationships before, and I watched him shut down. He pulled away immediately and said he understood that I needed something more than what he was offering. I felt guilty for giving him that ultimatum, but I knew I couldn't subject myself to this anymore. Once he began pulling away, I could feel myself coming after him. I had hoped that he would accept my ultimatum and give up the drugs to continue on with the connection that we had grown in just a few weeks. I didn't understand how two people could form such an instant connection and then give it all up for drugs. However, I was mistaking our connection for my sense of familiarity in the situation.

It was right before our reading break near the end of February that I stopped hearing from him. I hadn't expected this to turn around on me, and I felt the rejection hard. I had felt so vulnerable with him over the past few weeks because of the familiarity to being with Ben, and now he was rejecting me because I wasn't willing to accept the addictive behaviors.

That reading break, I went into a deep depression. My thoughts were consumed with confusion over the fact that someone could just cut one out of their life just like that. I knew I had proposed the ultimatum, but I really hadn't expected him to shut me out as quickly as he did. Even though we had only known each other for just a few weeks, I still felt a bond to him in my illogical mind. I was reliving a part of my past all over again which is why I struggled to let go of it. Maybe I could have changed the ending to this love story. I thought there might be a chance he might choose me over the drugs, but I was wrong. I would think about him all day long and try to distract myself from my thoughts that were giving me a million excuses as to why he wasn't feeling the same way about me. I was too consumed in the emotional affair I had made up in my head because of all the similarities he'd had to my late husband. It wasn't normal or healthy.

Every few days I would text and try to have some sort of contact, but it was no use. He would go AWOL, which I learned very quickly he did while he was using. The behaviors were all too familiar. I became obsessed with trying to reach out for him in some way, that I began using cocaine again in order to find some common ground. I thought that if he knew I was using, he might consider working things out because I had caved to his own addiction. I wasn't even aware of what I was doing to myself. After all the hard work I had put in over the past two months, I was still willing to push aside my boundaries and morals to avoid dealing with the painful rejection. There was still no response even though I had made it clear to him that I was again using, and that I was a hypocrite for putting those limitations on him. I was embarrassed that I was reaching out in this way, but I felt desperate. I was desperately longing to hold onto something that I'd lost all over again but wasn't even there to begin with. It wasn't until months later that I realized my desperation derived from old feelings and emotions I had felt when Ben had chosen alcohol and drugs over me. I was reliving this pain and didn't even see the common effects it had on me. The rejection from choosing substance abuse over me had made me feel vulnerable and had made me become a completely different person in that time. It made me ignore all the self-work I had done, and I was foolishly chasing after the pain and desertion I had once felt but hadn't emotionally dealt with.

Eventually, the weeks passed and so did our semester. I was relieved to be finished with the year and was preparing to continue with summer schooling. I was planning to do as many courses as I could through the summer and finish my second year in the fall semester. I would graduate in December, and from there, I had no plans other than to officially quit Chop and get a job where I would be happy to utilize my new skills and knowledge. As my uncle gave us our notice that spring to move out since he was planning to relist the condo, I planned to move into my dad's house where I could live for cheap rent and try to save. I wanted to work the least amount possible, as I was scheduled to take more classes through the summer and fall months. I was a little hesitant to move to my dad's because I knew he was drinking a lot more than what he was before, but I hadn't really known to what extent.

The weekend before I was planning to move, I had a little extra time on my hands now that school was done for a few weeks before my summer semester and I didn't have many shifts scheduled. A friend of mine had reached out and said he was in town for a little while since it was spring break up. He worked in the oil patch in Alberta and was off work for a couple months while there was no work during the spring. He was a good friend of Steven's and one of my best friends had dated him while Steven and I dated. We had stayed friends throughout the years and had communicated on and off. He was hanging out at the beach and invited me to come join him and catch up. I went and met him, and we caught up as old friends would. It was refreshing to see a familiar face after it had been so long.

The next few weeks, we were attached at the hip. He took me riding on his quad into the hills. We went for dinners and spent our time with friends and family. I had never considered him to be a romantic partner for me, but more as just a good friend. As the weeks went on, I started to recognize traits in him that I had always wanted in a partner. A couple months prior, as part of my manifestation process, I had written in my journal my top twenty qualities that I wanted in a partner. I took this page out of my journal and kept it in a drawer in my bedroom dresser with nothing else in it but the note. This empty drawer with just the note was intended for the Universe to bring someone to me that possessed all these qualities, and the empty drawer was sitting waiting to be filled. Many of these characteristics I already knew about him, but hadn't recognized in a romantic sense, but the more time I spent with him, the more I realized not only did he possess many of the qualities I had written down, but so many more that were on my list. The crazy part of it all was that Bart had intentions of coming back from Alberta on his spring break up to sweep me up and try to win me over. Before he left his rig, he was determined to see if there was anything more than friendship that could eventually grow into something romantic. I had never known that he had an interest in me even that prior Christmas while I briefly saw him, and I wouldn't find out until much later. It wasn't long though before we had established a romantic connection that spring.

Chapter 13

The winter semester was finished, and it would only be weeks before my summer classes began. I had been living with my dad for the past couple weeks already and planned to stay with him until I graduated in December of that year. Bart and I were spending every day together, mostly outdoors, going quadding, camping, and taking the boat out with my dad. I was starting to call in sick at work so I could spend more time with him. I wasn't exactly doing any studying but came up with excuse after excuse because I just couldn't bring myself to go into work while I was having so much fun. This was exactly the kind of relationship that I had been manifesting from the beginning of the year. He was stable, reliable and wasn't involved in any kinds of drugs.

I had expressed how much I didn't like the serving industry, and he wasn't complaining when I called in sick to spend more time with him. The weeks went on, and eventually I began summer classes at the beginning of June. Bart would drop me off at the college, pick me up, and bring me back to my dad's, where we would spend most of our evenings. Eventually, he began moving in some clothes and belongings, and before we knew it, he had basically moved in. We knew it would only be temporary because he would have to go back to work near the end of June, but we relished in the time that we were able to spend together.

There was no chaos and turmoil like my previous relationships all had been and I was beginning to see a real future with this relationship. Even though he wasn't working and had all the free time in the world, he was still right there by my side those entire two months. We spent time at his family's house, with my family and together alone getting to know each other better.

Finally, the end of June came upon us, and he received the call we had both been anticipating. He would need to be back at work within the week to start up again as the nicer weather had been approaching. He would be working in a small town in northern BC called Fort St. John which was about a twelve hour drive.

His drive back to work that day was the first time that we had been apart for more than twelve hours straight. As he was driving through the night in the middle of nowhere, he couldn't stop thinking about what Ben might think with everything that had gone on the past two months. He decided to ask Ben if this was the right thing to be doing. He had met Ben before but we didn't get together very often, the three of us. Bart was concerned what Ben might think and needed some kind of confirmation or blessing in order to move forward with a clear conscience. As he asked out loud if this was the right thing he should be doing, out of nowhere, in the midnight sky shot a single firework that lit up the sky ahead. It was the nod of approval Bart needed in order to move ahead with his sincere intentions.

After Bart left, things slowly began to change. Since he wouldn't be there to distract me from my studies and work, I knew I would have to put in more hours, which I had been dreading for weeks. One of the main focuses of my meditations were manifesting a relationship that I would have a long-term future with who was financially stable and able to support me as I finished my studies. This was part of the work that I had learned over the last five months in order to change my thought process and to attract a different situation in my life. I knew I didn't want to continue working at the restaurant and my heart wasn't in it, but I wanted to be able to put all my focus and energy into my schooling. I was looking for a partner that I could start a future with that could provide me the financial support that I needed. I just didn't know who that was going to be until I reconnected with Bart.

The week before he left, he sat me down and told me to quit my job. I explained I couldn't afford it, but he reassured me he would take care of my monthly bills until I finished school in December and could get a job. I couldn't believe what I was hearing. After months of meditation and visualizing this, it was becoming a reality. I was immensely grateful and began to focus my meditation on my grades.

I was more focused on school and my spirituality than ever. I had begun working out more often, and I was spending a lot of time with a girlfriend of mine, Monika. I had other things to focus on now that our relationship wasn't at the forefront of each day, and I could focus a little bit more on myself. I had been missing this time for myself for a while now and was grateful to have it back. As the weeks went on, I was home more in between my classes, and I had given notice at Chop. I was no longer working there now that Bart had offered to support me throughout the rest of the school year. Once I was finished, I would get a job right away, and I could support myself by doing something that I was truly passionate about and wanted to do. I was extremely grateful that Bart had offered to support me and that I could finally leave my job without the financial stress.

With Bart being gone, and being home by myself more often, I began to notice the drinking patterns my dad had developed over the past couple months had intensified. I had noticed his drinking habits had increased but hadn't paid the attention to it that I was now. Dad was recently semi-retired as he had just sold his automotive business a few months prior. He had owned and ran the business for over 25 years when an Import auto dealer offered him an amount he couldn't refuse to buy his lot and building. He had been struggling to make ends meet for a few years as his addiction amplified and didn't want the financial burden any longer. He had 15 employees who ran the parts, sales, and service divisions and managed them all while trying to manage his alcohol addiction. It was finally catching up with him, and he couldn't handle the struggles of operating a business while battling his dependency on alcohol. Many nights I caught him passed out on the couch or passed out in the front seat of his vehicle while sitting in the driveway. It petrified me that when he drove drunk, he wouldn't be able to recall where he had gone, or how he had gotten there.

One morning, I awoke out of bed around 10 am and found him sitting at his home office desk with a glass of vodka and orange juice. This was a fairly common occurrence more recently, and there wasn't much I was going to be able to say or do at this point to stop it. He said he had been up for a couple hours working on "paperwork" as he guzzled his morning beverages. When he felt tired around noon, I watched him stumble his way back to bed for a nap. He arose at 3:00 pm and came out of the bedroom, confused why he had slept all the way until 3:00 pm from the night before. He hadn't remembered waking up in the morning to catch up on paperwork while guzzling back a few screwdrivers before heading back to bed.

One night, I had been at Monika's house for the afternoon and came back home, hearing my dad's voice and a female's voice in the master bedroom. I could hear muffled laughing and teasing, so I snuck quietly into my bedroom so they wouldn't hear me. My dad and his girlfriend had broken up, but I was curious who my dad would have brought home that evening. The woman, who I figured was most likely an escort, was with my dad in his bedroom and had no idea I had come into the house. I quickly packed up my overnight things and headed back down to Monika's to spend the night. I knew it was my dad's home and it wasn't like I had much say in what he was doing, but I knew I had to get out of there immediately before we all were in an uncomfortable situation with each other. I knew I would have to address it with my dad the next day in hopes that it would never happen again. I hurried down to Monika's to stay the night so I could avoid the situation at home. I knew dad was struggling and I had empathy to his circumstances he'd been dealing with. I wasn't ready to address him right away but I was keeping a close eye on him. I knew it would have been hypocritical of me to point out his dependency on alcohol when I had struggled with the same thing.

A few days later, I was heading down the hill from our house to the college, like I usually would on a weekday afternoon for a class and noticed my dad's car parked on the side of the road. On the way to our place, there is a lookout point where you can pull in that overlooks a golf course immediately below with views of the lake and mountains. It had always been one of my dad's favorite places to go sit and think, so I wasn't surprised when I pulled up to see his car parked there. I pulled up right beside him and I could see he had his eyes closed and his head was bobbing back and forth to the music he had cranked in his car. I knew he had been drinking and so I laid into my horn to try and make him realize I was parked beside him, ready to give him the gears. He didn't even blink. He was too out of it to recognize I was hovering in front of his window, and the music was too loud to hear the horn. I was angry and frustrated, so I debated with the idea of calling the police so they could give him some kind of wake-up call. I left the lookout point and it didn't take me long before I was dialing the station. I hadn't wanted my dad to know it was me that called him in, so I went on with my day, headed into class, and prepared myself for him to have his license suspended and to hear about it by the time I got home.

That evening, I came home to find him sitting in the living room, having a drink, and not seeming to care that he just had his license taken away again. He had just gotten his license back from having it suspended for a month not long before. It was before Bart had left back to work and he was driving his Porsche down to the liquor store that was only a five minute drive from the house. He was already into the liquor and shouldn't have been driving as he was flying down the road and lost control, which led him to hit a concrete block on the side of the road and crush the front end of his car. He was surprisingly not hurt and lucky that Bart was driving at the same time and saw him.

That day, Dad filled me in on the details of his day, saying that someone called him in, and the police came to take his vehicle away to the impound and brought him back home, where they would issue him a long-term suspension for driving under the influence. I was relieved to know that he would at least be off the roads in his condition, and I felt glad that wouldn't be something I would have to stress about for a while. As the weeks into summer went by, my stress levels had raised significantly as I watched my dad drink his way into a slow loneliness and desolation. I hadn't anticipated this to be causing my high levels of anxiety, but it was slowly rising and it felt like I was once again consumed with the addiction of someone I was living with.

With Dad losing his license, it was some sort of relief that I needed so I could get back to focusing on my studies and preparing myself to graduate at the end of the year. I only had five more months of school left before I completed my diploma, and the stress and anxiety I'd been feeling was hindering my focus.

It was mid-July, and hot as ever in the Okanagan. I was spending many of my weekday afternoons either studying in class or basking in the sunshine in the back yard with my books and laptop. One afternoon, while studying for a midterm that I had coming up, I began to sweat profusely, and a wave of nausea swept over me. It was so sudden and out of nowhere that I thought maybe I'd eaten something bad or had gotten too much sun. I had been sun tanning out in the yard for a while and wondered if I went inside into the air conditioning if I'd start feeling a bit better. I started the shower and hoped a little cool water would take this feeling away. It wasn't working, so I decided I might need to eat a little something. This physical feeling was extremely similar to when I had my anxiety attack back in 2009, although it wasn't quite as intense. I noticed my hearing was off, almost like I had water clogged in my eardrums or they were plugged. I also noticed that my balance seemed to be off a bit, and my depth perception was off. I didn't like this feeling at all, and I began to panic. I tried to talk myself down from the paralyzing fear that was creeping over me, but it was overtaking. My fears immediately went to the panic attack I'd previously had, and now I was all alone at the house. I tried to distract myself and get back to my work, but I just couldn't focus. I decided to go for a run, and it helped in the short term. It was nearly 35 degrees Celsius, and there was only so much running I could do on a hot afternoon. The only thing I could think of was to pour myself a stiff drink and hope that this feeling would subside. After a few drinks, it did, and I began to feel back to normal. It wasn't until the next morning that I woke up, felt fine for the first ten minutes, and then the feeling hit me again. It was beginning to scare me. I didn't like this out of body feeling and didn't like the fact that I couldn't focus and set my mind straight. I knew I had a limited amount of time to study for my midterms, and I didn't want this distraction to take away from it. I was also planning a trip to Fort St. John that next week to go stay with Bart for a few nights and hoped I would be feeling better by then. My plan was to drive myself the twelve hours to Northern BC and study while he worked during the day, and we would spend time together in the evenings. I had to get through my midterm first, so that week I focused as much as I possibly could while medicating my anxiety with alcohol in the evenings. It was a vicious cycle I couldn't get away from and it snuck up on me once again.

The morning I was ready to begin my twelve hour journey, I woke up at 4:30 am ready to hit the road, even though I knew it was going to be a long, lonely drive up North. I packed my things into the car, turned on my music and began the drive through the mountains. I was unfamiliar with the route I was taking, so I was already feeling uncomfortable that I didn't know my way. The feeling that I'd had for the past week crept over me once again as I tried to distract myself with recorded comedy sessions I'd downloaded to listen to on the drive. I noticed that my depth perception was still off, and it seemed like vehicles were sometimes nearer or further, then they were in reality. I couldn't figure it out. My hearing was off, and I was constantly trying not to panic as I continued on my journey. I tried not to stop, as I didn't want the trip to take any longer than it had to and I was all alone which made it worse for me. I had gone to see my doctor a few days before I left, and she instructed me to get some blood work done after I told her all of my symptoms. They said it would take a couple of days to get any results, so I would just have to be patient.

Without being familiar with the drive and not feeling like myself, I had a major fear that I would have a panic attack and be all by myself in a place I didn't know. I called as many people as I could on that drive, just to help me get through the hours. When I finally arrived in Fort St. John, I felt comforted that I was now with Bart, but I still needed alcohol to take the anxiety away. I didn't like the fact that I was needing to rely on alcohol, but it was a quick and easy fix. I wanted that normal feeling back again, and I hadn't had it for almost a week, other than when I was drinking. That entire week went by in a blur. I would wake up in the morning in the hotel room and it would feel like the room was closing in on me, or I would take a walk down unfamiliar roads, and I would feel lost and afraid. I tried studying at a coffee shop for a few hours throughout the day, but each time I would go there, I would feel even more pressure to get my schoolwork done, but too stressed out to get anything accomplished. I was too distracted trying to distract myself! I was so relieved when Bart would come back from work, and we could have a few drinks and I could take my mind off of my struggles throughout the day. I was patiently waiting for the phone call back from the Dr., and finally received a call a few days in. The doctor's office said that they couldn't release any information over the phone and that I would need to book an appointment with the doctor when I got back into town. I booked an appointment for the week that I was back home to get some answers. I thought I would hopefully feel better after hearing from the doctor, however this wait only spiked my anxiety even more. I began to spiral and self-diagnose every illness and disease I could think of that might relate to the symptoms I was having. I went into panic mode, and I noticed my symptoms started getting worse. We were on our way out into the bush to do some quadding and I noticed my right ear seemed to be slightly deaf. It was like I had no hearing in my ear and it would go in and out of feeling this way. I can remember covering my left ear and trying to listen with my right, only to hear blurred sounds. This went on for the rest of my stay, and I was almost relieved to be leaving to go back home to find out what exactly was going on. I was extremely tired and drained from the stress I had felt all week, but also dreading the drive home on my own. I had wondered if maybe my iron levels were extremely low, so I stocked up on beef jerky and anything I could get my hands on that I thought was high in iron. I was irrational and couldn't connect the dots that possibly the drinking was the main factor in contributing to my wearing anxiety.

Halfway through the trip home, I felt extremely tired and knew I needed to take a nap break. I stopped at a rest stop where I went in to refuel on beef jerky. As I waited in line at the counter, a wave of dizziness swept through me, and I had to physically balance myself against the counter. I started going in and out of a blackout and quickly gathered myself as I groggily paid for my meat and left. I went straight to my car to stretch out my seat and try to take a nap. I couldn't take much more of the lightheaded waves and tried to rest. After a half hour of unsuccessful nap time, I decided to get back on the road to end my journey as quickly as I could. I had to constantly talk myself out of feeling like I was going to pass out and count down the miles it would take to reach my mom's house, where I would be safe. When I finally arrived at my moms, I was completely exhausted and mentally drained from being in panic mode for twelve hours straight. I looked forward to getting some answers that next week and to do whatever I needed to do in order to get myself feeling back to normal.

That next week, I was back in class and had my appointment at the doctor's office. My anxiety was still at an all-time high. I felt extremely anxious thinking about how I would make it through three-hour lectures while fighting off the symptoms I'd been experiencing for the past few weeks.

The day I went into the doctor's office I was feeling unprepared as I expected to receive some bad news. I kept thinking over and over in my mind of the different symptoms I'd been experiencing and couldn't pinpoint exactly what it could be but felt like I needed to hear some answers regardless of what it was. When I went in, I felt foolish when she told me that I had been experiencing severe anxiety. My blood work had all come back normal and there was no definitive signs of anything physically wrong. I was stunned because that hadn't even crossed my mind, regardless of what I had been through in the past couple years, let alone months. She explained to me that I had been on a constant level of high anxiety and that I was basically in anxiety attack mode straight for the past few weeks. I'd never experimented this amount of anxiety, so I just assumed that even with the physical symptoms I was having, it had to be some sort of disease or illness I was suffering from. She advised me that I should go back on medication immediately, as I had been off it for a while, and she wrote me a prescription and offered me an anxiety class that might help which was through the Interior Health division that would be covered for me to attend. It was a six-week class, and it would teach me skills and tips on how to cope with anxiety. I filled the prescription immediately after I left and signed up for the class. I was ready to feel back to normal again and to get my life back on track. I knew it would take at least three weeks for the medication to kick in and to start feeling better, so I decided that I would try to spend as much time in my room away from the stress and discomfort so I could focus on my schoolwork and try to separate myself from the chaos that was inside my home.

That next week, I went in for my midterm exam and I could feel the nerves kicking in when I sat down in the room. I could feel the room closing in on me, and my hearing seemed to fade. I immediately became anxious and needed to get up to go to the bathroom to regain myself and talk myself down. I knew the medication hadn't kicked in yet, but I knew that once I began to focus on my studies, the distractions of my mind would calm me down. I got through my exam and felt confident as I was leaving. There was something about numbers and mathematics that seemed to distract me and made me focus only on the task at hand. I had been majoring in accounting and the classes required for me to graduate were difficult but interesting and kept my mind occupied. For that, I was grateful.

That week, I tried to focus more on my studies, and tried to keep to myself in my room. I usually laid in my bed in the evenings, watching television or doing homework, and I would continue to indulge in a few glasses of wine. The alcohol was a contributing factor to my anxiety, but I wasn't willing to give up the only few hours that would calm my relentless mind. The week after my midterms, I knew I was able to relax a little more on the studying but had less of a distraction in the evenings without my study sessions. I had the relief of hoping I would start to feel better in the next couple weeks. As I was lying in bed one evening, feeling accomplished that I had completed my midterms, I was startled by a stabbing pain in the center of my chest. It nearly took my breath away as it was so sudden and out of nowhere. I'd never had such a strong sensation before, even though it wasn't all that painful. The most frightening part was that it was a stabbing pain in the very center of my chest, and it concerned me because I thought maybe I was having a heart attack. The stabbing sensations were concerning because they came out of nowhere and I hadn't considered them to be one of my anxiety symptoms since I had never experienced them before. I was too afraid to be home by myself, so I got out of bed, packed an overnight bag and went down to Monika's. She lived right around the corner from the hospital where she brought me to, because I wasn't sure what to do. It was 10:00 by the time we got to the emergency room, where we waited to see the doctor for an EKG scan. I was positive it was something serious, because I'd never quite experienced these physical symptoms ever before. The doctor ran the tests and nothing came back out of the ordinary. I explained to him my other symptoms I had had for the past few weeks, and he concluded that it was chest pain from anxiety. I couldn't believe the amount of physical symptoms my body had been experiencing but was relieved to know that it was anxiety and once my medication began to kick in, it would help settle them. It was two in the morning by the time I left the hospital, and Monika had already gone back to her house as she had to work early the next morning. She lived about two blocks down the road from the hospital, so I decided I could walk, and I would call Bart on the way. I was explaining to him what happened at the hospital as I was turning the corner onto her street. I was coming up to her house when I noticed a man crouching down under a short shrub, and he looked to be hiding from something or someone. It startled me, and my heart started pounding. It was the house directly across the street from Monika's, and I couldn't get in the door fast enough. It was another shock to my nervous system that ended the night in exhaustion after being in the hospital until two in the morning.

The rest of the summer went by quickly as I began to feel the effects of my medication kicking in and I was starting to feel a lot better. Bart and I had been discussing moving to Alberta at the end of the year when I finished my diploma, and he would work for a different company where he could be a little closer to home than in Fort. St. John which was where he'd been for years. I knew we had just started dating in April, but everything about our relationship felt right. Even though I was a widow at the age of 23 and had been through so much already at my age, I felt confident in our relationship that it was something that would last. It was the most stability that I had ever felt in my entire life. I began looking at house rentals in the city we planned to move to in Alberta and felt out the market. We were planning a trip out to Edmonton in September for one of Bart's cousin's weddings, and we planned to make a trip south of Edmonton to Red Deer to scope out the city. Bart had lived there years before while he was working for another company in the service rig industry and had always liked it, so it was an easy choice. While we were there, we would check out the different areas in town and decide which area we liked best and aim to find a place there by the beginning of Jan. 2013.

In the fall, I began my final semester, in which I would complete in December and would graduate as a Business Admin Diploma graduate with a major in accounting. I knew I couldn't allow any distractions as we had come to the agreement that we would be officially moving to Alberta at the end of the Semester, and I would begin looking for work as finals were approaching. We spent two days in Red Deer after the wedding we attended for Bart's cousin, and we found a townhome that we fell in love with and began the process of applying for our first home together. By the time I arrived back in Kelowna, I was determined to stick to my studies, begin getting familiar with job opportunities and prepare to complete the rest of the year with a handle on my anxiety. By then, my anxiety had immensely calmed down and I was extremely relieved that I was beginning to feel back to my normal self again. I had been meditating weekly on getting my anxiety under control and the meditations brought me a sense of calming and peace. I knew the spirituality and medications were working hand in hand to bring me back to my normal self.

That fall, there was still one major factor that was contributing to my anxiety, which was my dad's drinking habits that hadn't reduced by any means. I was noticing that as the months went on, he was getting deeper and deeper into a depression, and I noticed I was having the same chest pains I was having in the summer. I was able to distract myself when Bart was on days off from work and we would be out of the house for the most part, but we both noticed Dad was getting worse. I can recall Bart and I lying in bed one evening watching a movie, when I heard my dad pull into the driveway. He sat in his vehicle for an hour before I heard the car door close. The garage door opened, and we heard a loud crashing noise. I jolted out of bed and sprinted to the garage door to find my dad's legs up in the air horizontally, and his body had fallen into the cardboard box of recycling. I rushed over to help him up, but he could barely walk on his own. We brought him into the house and stood him in the laundry room so we could help him take off his shoes and coat. He couldn't stand on his own and kept swaying, catching his balance on the wall or the washing machine. He told us to leave him be, and he would make his way to his room, on his own. We went back to the room, left the door open so we could hear him, and eventually he began his crawl past our bedroom on hands and knees to his room where he would pull himself up onto the bed and pass out. I couldn't imagine how he had even made it home driving while in this state when he couldn't even hold himself up and make it to his bed. This behavior became so immune to me after so many months of experiencing and living with it, that I hadn't recognized how this affected me and my anxiety.

The fall continued on, as I crammed for midterms in mid-October, and I continued to watch my dad drink his life away. I began cooking for him because he would go days without eating a full meal. I would go to class and come home late in the afternoon to find him swaying about in the kitchen or passed out on the couch with the TV left on and an empty glass falling out of his hands. As Bart and I planned our move to Red Deer at the end of December, I began worrying about who was going to take care of my dad if something didn't change. He would be living alone when I left, and that was a major concern of mine. By November, I started reaching out to my mom, who had gone through this five years prior, and she pointed me in the direction of the same company she hired to do an intervention on my dad the first time. I was put into contact with Darren at Axis Intervention Services, and he was a huge support for what I was dealing with firsthand. I explained to him in detail what had been going on for the past few months and how my dad's drinking had escalated tenfold in the past couple months, even, just over the summer, and how it had affected me. I expressed my concerns that when I left, there would be no one to check on him on a daily basis, and I was worried that he would spiral even further. I knew if I didn't do something, he would eventually die of alcoholism. I had seen it once before, and I wasn't prepared to leave the province without trying everything I could to get him some help. Darren suggested that we do another intervention on Dad, and I was hesitant because of how the last intervention turned out. When my mom organized the first intervention for my dad back in 2007, he was not happy about it and only agreed to go to treatment for my mom's sake. He didn't do it for himself, which in turn spiked the relapse, and I was afraid that the same situation might happen again. I couldn't bear the thought of a relapse that might end up being worse than it already was. In treatment, they say that alcohol is a progressive disease, which makes sense because Dad's drinking had progressed exponentially even in just a few months. I spoke with my sisters and my mom, and we all agreed that this was the right move to make. If we didn't do something drastic, there was no hope for his recovery in the future, so we agreed that we would do an intervention in December before Christmas. Darren had a few options for treatment centers that he thought Dad might agree to, and I had lined up everything for the morning we scheduled the intervention. Darren would come to our house in the morning before Dad got up, and I would have my sisters there also. My one sister lived in Vancouver, so we would Skype with her so she would be included in the process. It was December and I was studying for finals, preparing to make one of the biggest moves in my life and planning to send my dad to a treatment center for his alcohol addiction all within weeks of itself.

The morning of the intervention, as we sat around him like we had five years ago and read our letters we each had written, Dad had agreed to get the help he needed. I couldn't believe the relief I felt. He agreed to leave in a few days once he got a few things in order because he didn't know how long he would be away for. I felt overwhelmed and relieved all at the same time. After months of watching him fade into this desolation and misery, he would finally have some hope for a better life. I had seen him at his very worst; as he leaned over the kitchen sink, mumbling and stumbling, crashing into doorways, windows, and kitchen cabinets, and crawling when he didn't have the strength to walk. This was my final chance at attempting to do my part and get him some help, and it had paid off.

Those next few days didn't slow him down any; in fact, I think he was trying to get in his last bit of alcoholic freedom before he would have to detox. While he continuously drank, he booked himself into a treatment center in Hawaii called Hawaii Island Recovery in Kailua-Kona. A few days later, he was packed and ready to begin his new journey as we sent him off to his new life of sobriety as he stumbled his way onto the plane.

Chapter 14

We made the big move to Alberta on December 28th, 2012. We were scheduled to get the keys to our new home on the 29th, and I would start work on the first Monday after New Year's Day. I had applied for a bookkeeping position online and was offered a job after a successful Skype interview. It was a brand-new city, which meant brand new friends and new opportunities, and I was excited about it, yet nervous. It was time for me to leave my past behind and create new beginnings for my future. I knew it would be a good move for me, mentally and spiritually.

Since Dad had agreed to go to treatment to get the help he so desperately needed, that was one less thing for me to worry about. Mom was back with my stepdad and had been for months now, which was a relief that there was also some stability there. My two younger sisters had planned on moving out to Alberta, eventually also which gave me some comfort that I wouldn't be all alone in a new town where I knew no one.

The decision to move happened at the right time. My new job was a perfect fit for what I was looking for and was challenging yet rewarding. It was my opportunity to start fresh and begin again to create a circle of friends that I could trust for support and lean on. I was in a position where I could create a future for myself that I truly wanted. I had a partner who supported me in everything I did and would never let me down. I began to understand what trust meant in a partner. I began to understand what a healthy environment finally looked and felt like. It was something I had been needing and craving for so long; stability, consistency and the permanence I sought after in my meditations. For months, I had put in the work in order to get to where I was and I knew that I was the one who created this new reality.

I began to seek additional spiritual awareness as I began to settle into a routine of calm and uniformity. As my strength and spirit grew, my mindset became my power. I had learned over the past year what it took to turn my visions into realities. I relied on my spirituality as my strength to move forward. Finally, I had found my longing for what was missing in my life for so long.

As I began to adopt new habits and rituals, I became more and more aware of the fact that I was creating my own existence. More opportunities came my way and better solutions to problems. I was learning to deal with any issues from the past in a positive and effective way.

Shortly after, I was introduced to the book "The Magic" by Rhonda Byrnes, which taught me my journey to gratitude. I felt a yearning for more depth and direction, and this was the next step for me. Over the course of 28 days, I practiced gratitude in a way that I never had before. This was even more of a mindset shift for me as I began looking at negative things in my life in a more positive way. I learned to appreciate the challenges or strains in my life as I educated myself on the teachings that they were there to make me grow stronger as a person and to learn lessons from them.

These were life lessons that no one could teach me, other than myself. Once I moved and saw the results of my powerful mind at work, I adopted these habits into my everyday life. I began a journey of soul work, and after many years practicing this I noticed the synchronicities and affirmations that I was indeed on the right path. I knew that the struggles I had endured had created me into the person I now had become. I couldn't see it at the time, but I see it clearly now.

My dad's sobriety from treatment had finally made an impact on his life in which he was able to sustain for the past ten years and counting. In 2015, Bart and I got married, and in 2017 I birthed a beautiful baby girl. Amidst the 2020 global pandemic, we also became legal guardians of my ten-year-old nephew. The pandemic affected millions of people and hit my sister while in quarantine, who had been sober for months. She had been to a treatment center a few years prior but struggled as her addiction suffered once again through the isolation that the pandemic enforced upon us. Thus began her roller coaster of binges which sent her back to rehab. Maddy spent four months in the same treatment center my dad and Ben had gone to and received the treatment she had needed for self-recovery and rehabilitation. She now has her son back and is strong in her recovery after two years.

I can say openly and honestly that there have been many challenging times as my spirituality grows and there had been times where I questioned my faith. However, when I put into practice all that I have learned throughout the years, it always brings me back to a place of grounding and mindfulness that it is only up to me to create what I desire.

I have experienced so much fear in the past throughout my traumas and travesties, because I never had the conviction to get me through. I can honestly say that I am grateful to have the knowledge that I acquired and the willingness to continue on the path of spiritual awareness and mindfulness. I wouldn't say that I don't have my doubts and fears that arise when circumstances happen which have a negative impact on my life, but I try to put faith in the fact that there is a reason for everything, and we are here to live and to learn through these experiences in order to gain knowledge and fulfillment in this lifetime.